WHAT IS THE GOSPEL TRUTH?

WHAT IS THE GOSPEL TRUTH?

IS THERE ANYTHING WE CAN TRUST?

ALEXANDER WOOLLEY

Matador
Unit E2 Airfield Business Park,
Harrison Road, Market Harborough,
Leicestershire. LE16 7UL
Tel: 0116 2792299
Email: books@troubador.co.uk
Web: www.troubador.co.uk/matador
Twitter: @matadorbooks

ISBN 978 1805140 009

British Library Cataloguing in Publication Data.
A catalogue record for this book is available from the British Library.

Printed and bound in Great Britain by 4edge Limited
Typeset in 12pt Caslon Pro by Troubador Publishing Ltd, Leicester, UK

Matador is an imprint of Troubador Publishing Ltd

This book is dedicated to Margaret and anyone else who reads with a generous mind and a critical eye.

CONTENTS

—

ONE   1

Evidence for the existence and character of Jesus and the style of his ministry is examined, while the importance of this, with regard to the multiplicity of current faiths, is also emphasised.

TWO   12

Particular changes, additions or disjunctions in the three Gospels described as synoptic are singled out as examples of what we should look for to discover the likely truth, while some events are explained in a way that might seem more acceptable to those who want accounts which follow scientific or experiential principles. The real burden of what Jesus taught is deduced. The character and credibility of the resurrection is examined while the character of eternal life and existence of hell, as touted at present around the world, are questioned.

SIX 186

Gospel truths on which we may rely.

ACKNOWLEDGEMENTS
AND PREFACE

—

I have not had the help of any theological scholar to correct mistakes or produce any better ideas or improve those I have tried to develop: I neither move in, nor belong to, such circles. I have had only the valuable help of the scholarship of the proofreader, Gareth Vaughan, whose expertise is more in other disciplines. I remain deeply indebted to his meticulous care and the very high standard of his work. One may, therefore, anticipate errors in this book which will be due only to me but whose presence does not, itself, invalidate the general line of thinking nor the burden of the argument; there will also be occasions when valuable points have not been made. I am merely a messenger, who believes that he has somehow been gradually given, during a period of more than eight decades, an important message to deliver, even if some of the 'words' in the message are inadequate or wrong, which will be in spite of frequent revision and subsequent correction.

I have sometimes been asked who my intended readers might be. The answer I offer is that the hoped-for audience is those who are open-minded and feel some cause for doubt, while they want also to discover trustworthy evidence for some religious belief. This potential audience of interested agnostics is now, I believe, large, while in today's world, where people have rapid access to information through the internet, accuracy and credibility are important; this internet information may be inaccurate on occasion, but it has been supplied, for the most part, in good faith.

Too many religious claims, currently, seem to be bedevilled by daunting implausibility the moment one 'digs below the surface': the faith which they purport to embody may, on deeper acquaintance, appear less satisfactory than originally expected. Firm foundations for religious faith are now needed and this book is an attempt to find and establish these.

INTRODUCTION

—

The raison d'être of this book is to introduce what may be different ways of searching for new arguments which support the possibility of there being truth in the belief that God directed Jesus during his ministry, as well as reinforcing those arguments which try to demonstrate that other forms of existence, different from what we ourselves experience in this material world, are conceivable. The propositions in this book will not be popular with every believer in the truth of Jesus's message. I am trying to explain how later additions appear to have masked the truth and I am using possibly different ways by which to establish those tenets which may be regarded as logically sustainable. It is intended for the many who are at present 'uncommitted' rather than for the more select few who are already 'committed'.

To be described as committed it is not enough to say that one follows prescribed rituals in perfunctory fashion: one must be more than perfunctorily tepid; one must be involved 'heart and soul' in everything which the ritual entails. One may read on p. 388 in Barclay's commentary on Mark (St Andrews Press, 1956) about the one who *knows about* Jesus and the one who *knows* Jesus. How many feel fully the meaning of the Lord's Prayer as they recite those traditional – or, nowadays, not always so traditional – words? If we mean 'Hallowed be thy name', when we recite those words, we do not at any time show disrespect for that name in an unthinking exclamation. It is suspected that many who attend religious services and functions have not much more real, living trust in the basis of what they profess to believe than had the average Classical Roman or Greek in the traditional Gods and myths of their times. How many, for instance, feel that 'God is there' ready to direct them every moment of their lives?

Mark's Gospel says (2:21 & 22): "No one sews a patch of new cloth, which has not been shrunk already, onto an old piece of clothing [woollen material which has been shrunk as well as weakened by washing and wear], else the new patch tears away leaving a larger hole, just as one avoids putting new wine into old wineskins, as the new wine would burst the old skins and all would be lost." What is said in this book might be like that new patch, which has not been shrunk by adequate critical appraisal, or even like rough unpalatable new wine from a vineyard without any repute, which will damage old, established ways of thinking and believing: many of us may feel safely sure of the divine source of the teaching of Jesus and those who are comfortably settled in their own individual ways of thinking about Jesus and God might feel that the arguments in this book could weaken some of the foundations of those beliefs; on the other hand, if these people feel they should spread the message of Jesus, it is of great importance that what they spread is not only right but also convincing.

As was pointed out in the first of my earlier books ('A New Vision', Matador, 2021, p. 23), an important proportion of first and second century written material has been lost since the time of Jesus. Further, as Jesus was not seen as an important person then, except by his disciples, most of whom will have been illiterate, and later converts, the majority of whom will have been illiterate also, there were relatively few records about him anyway. Most of the surviving contemporary records are in the writings only of those who considered Jesus divine. There are a few exceptions; among these are the Babylonian Talmud, a Jewish record, whose reference to Jesus is thought by many not to refer to the Jesus of the Gospels, which suffered some censorship at the hands of both Jews and Christians, and the texts of Suetonius Tranquillus, which were not, as far we know, interfered with by Christians. It should be noted that Ian Wilson, on p. 62 of 'Jesus: the Evidence', (Weidenfeld and Nicolson, 1984) adduces evidence to show that this reference in the Babylonian Talmud *does* refer to the Jesus of the Gospels, while John Ashton, on p. 214 of the second edition of 'Understanding the Fourth Gospel' (OUP, 2007) clearly thinks it does too. There are also the works of Cornelius Tacitus, who thought the new religion a pernicious superstition, and Flavius Josephus, both of whose texts seem to have suffered from some Christian interference. These two latter authors refer to the crucifixion of Jesus as being at the orders of Pontius Pilate. When Josephus refers to Jesus as no more than a wise man, one may be fairly confident that this was from the pen of Josephus himself rather than a later addition from a Christian redactor.

A further problem is that the writers of the books which make up the New Testament were very enthusiastic supporters of the cause they were promoting. They were totally convinced of its truth. Thucydides may have belittled Herodotus, the father of History (which meant 'Enquiry'), as not being reliable because he was keen to attract a paying audience: it was more important for him to be interesting, Thucydides had imagined, than to be completely accurate. Herodotus may have been more entertaining than Thucydides, but he seems to have tried very hard to be accurate at the same time. Thucydides claimed he had written a 'ktema es aei' (possession for always) but

Herodotus has too. However, the Gospel writers would have paid little attention to this, even if they had known about it, because their view of the truth was far more important in their eyes than anything else. They may not have been seeking to make any money but they were not at all unbiassed either. They will have compiled their contributions, interpreting the data and adding conjectural additions, as fitted their beliefs. They will have tended to discard any data which did not support their message, even though, most fortunately, they did not always do so. When we read their works, we need to try to identify those particular accounts where their bias may, by omission, alteration or addition, have resulted in distortion of the underlying truth; we may then try to recover the true facts. Even more important are those occasions when what they have recorded is contrary to the picture they wanted their readers to see, and, just as important, those occasions when they have obviously misinterpreted the data they have come across.

Because there survives only a small quantity of unbiassed material which covers the early years of 'Christianity', we cannot establish as much as we might wish with any certainty. However, it is argued here that, in spite of the problems, a useful amount may still be worked out by examining the records which do survive. One has only to analyse carefully what is said, trying to identify possible sources and any signs of tampering, so as to establish some very helpful indications. This may not accord with the criteria by which the suitability of evidential data is assessed nowadays but, in a matter as important as this, we should use whatever data are available, and use them as productively as we can manage.

Underlying all this there is the proposition that there are important truths hidden by fanciful decorations, in the fashion of a decorated Christmas tree; the tree that is the story of the ministry of Jesus is true, it is real, it happened, although it was plainer and more straightforward than the decorations and subsequent additional beliefs now portray. However beautiful, however alluring, these additions may be in their present guise, these distracting fruits of human fancy are often misleading and damaging. There may be no need to have all these decorations thrown away permanently, but one does need to have them removed, at least temporarily, so as properly to see the reality which underlies it all; many of the decorations may be put back afterwards, provided one continues to remember the basic truths which are the foundations of what one should believe.

This may be put another way: a hymn by George Herbert contains the verse:

A man that looks on glass,
On it may stay his eye,
Or, if he pleaseth, through it pass
And then the heaven espy.

I have tried to look at the scenery on the other side of the glass. It seems that many commentators have not bothered or managed to see what is on the other side of the glass. This is what I have tried to do. The 'glass wall' (rather than glass ceiling) seems to have made reconsidering or questioning the reliability of the evidence, as it is presented in the New Testament, taboo.

The importance of establishing the truth about Jesus, and his relationship to God, is becoming ever more significant. There have been assaults on Judaic beliefs, as well as on all other religious belief, by people who have found parts of the creeds or scripture insufficiently supported by internal logic or external experience – one may think of Professors Alfred Ayer and Richard Dawkins, although there are very many others. Here is an example of atheistic argument: 'Saying that there is anything good about Christianity is like saying that Hitler was kind to his dog [did Hitler have one? Why not kind to Eva Braun, which sounds a little more feasible?]. If someone is a sadistic, violent burglar, but a charmer with the people he meets in the street, does this charm make up for the rest of his behaviour? Christianity, and other religions for that matter, have been responsible for the most appalling acts. Because of this, religion should be regarded with disdain and blamed for much of mankind's unhappiness.' This argument omits the egregiously cruel regimes which are fuelled by atheism. Such a mind could be conceived as proposing that the decision of an apparently sane but, in fact, mentally deranged, and very dangerous, individual to inflict death and destruction on the innocent people of Ukraine, was Christian in principle and practice. Fifteen minutes, or less, spent studying the actual teaching of Jesus, would correct such unjustifiable ideas; or they might look at Isaiah 11:1-9, where one sees the words: "They will neither harm nor destroy on all my holy mountain, for the earth will be full of the knowledge of the Lord, as the waters cover (and fill the bed of) the sea."

The refusal to look at all the available evidence dispassionately, most disappointingly commands many an atheist's blinkered view of life. The deliberate vacuum in their minds has sucked in debilitating fantasies which destroy any chance of effective thinking. The confusion spawned by people using demonstrably illogical arguments is the foundation stone of the fortress of disbelief which is these atheists' religion. Such arguments need to be addressed and answered adroitly; for instance, illogically equating creeds with people, as in the extract above, is an elementary mistake which needs to be dealt with very early on, as it derails attempts properly to reason. The proposition that any *good* deed on the part of someone who is guilty of grave misdemeanours is of no use, is as foolish as arguing that legitimate money from an evil-doer should not be used for the benefit of those who need help. If the result of a past ill can be used for a present good, that should be greeted with joy. One may not be able to change the past but one can often make the present and future better. Every good deed is to be welcomed, whoever may be the doer; one good deed may well lead to another; reform or metanoia in the ill-intentioned people of this world is what we should all seek, and their doing good, rather than ill, helps bring this about.

It is what Jesus actually taught which is important. He made it quite clear that violence against people in any form was to be avoided. Any regime that practises violence, torture and murder is satanic, whatever the claims may be. The current regimes (2023) in Iran and Afghanistan are not being guided by our loving creator God, as their leaders might seem to claim. These regimes are satanic. The same should be said of so-called Christian regimes that practised violence, torture and murder in the past; these, too, were satanic.

One might remember that it is the possession of an open mind that marks out a successful academic, particularly a brilliant scientist. Interestingly, the female of our species, being genetically more alert to surprising change, seems to provide fewer closed-mind atheists than does the male variety. Perhaps ladies enjoy a valuable advantage.

There are also many people now who have become uncertain about what may be believed with any confidence. Some of them need help to discover the truth which is there, but which has not yet been identified clearly enough for them to be persuaded they can trust it. This means that those who spread a message need to be sure that all the details in that message are right and none of it mere hear-say or unsubstantiated fancy. If any component of a message is dubious or wrong, there will be doubt in the minds of some about the validity of the rest of the message; if more than one item is dubious or wrong, the doubt and the number of doubters will be greater. One must remember too, that an enormous amount of information and expert opinion is available on the internet and that will not allow unfounded claims to have as much chance of gaining general acceptance as they had in the past. When something is of considerable importance, many people, nowadays, want to be certain that what they are being asked to believe is warranted by evidence and argument.

There are some decorations which may be thrown away as little more useful than rotting rubbish: if one were to read Charles Wesley's hymn, 'Gentle Jesus, meek and mild', one might remember that Jesus overthrew the tables of the money changers in the Temple precincts and preached very vigorously against the religious slavery laid upon all Jews then by the complicated demands of the scribal interpretation of the law. The conduct of Jesus during his arrest, then before the High Priest and afterwards during the trial before Pilate and subsequent crucifixion, demonstrated monumental courage and unwavering determination. Jesus might have been gentle, meek and mild sometimes, especially with women and children, but, with his seemingly irrepressible sense of humour and imperturbable courage, he was, rather more often, other very different things too.

A useful example of how a false decoration may come to be fashioned is the way in which the descent of Jesus from David is chronicled in Matthew and Luke. It is quite clear that the line of descent which they choose to follow is the one through Joseph, his declared father, when the two writers are claiming, with the 'same pen', that Joseph was not really the father, but that God was, via the Holy Spirit, through Mary, for whom no genealogy is furnished. If Joseph was not the real father, there was no point whatever in producing these very fanciful and apparently contrived genealogies. Jesus was almost inevitably 'born of David' anyway, even if some of the progenitors in the line of descent were female rather than the 'prescribed' only male, as every true Jew alive in the time of Jesus was almost inevitably descended from David. The requirements for those claiming to be a true Jew, then, were restrictive and rigidly applied: they were all sons of David, just as they were all sons of God. The writers of Matthew and Luke calculated their genealogies, using what they could discover in the Old Testament, without, as far as we can tell, recourse to any other reliable evidential source, and then used their discoveries to support lines of descent which were logically irrelevant to what they were trying to establish. Indeed, Luke's taking the line of descent back to the mythical Adam vitiates any possible respect for its reliability. Any religion that treats of Adam as historical, rather than symbolic, invites doubt as to its credentials. This process demonstrates clearly the way in which the writers of Matthew and Luke often worked to fill the very numerous gaps in the evidence.

It is quite possible that people had begun to fashion these extra decorations even before the crucifixion; but the process of invention and variety of product has certainly gathered pace since then and seems to be continuing still in the rambling rooms of the Vatican and Lambeth Palace, as well as in numerous articles, in books, in lectures and in many of the pulpits around the world. In November, 2022, a 'sermon' given in Cambridge was addressing the appearance of Jesus's crucifixion wounds in mediaeval paintings and their similarities with female anatomical attributes. There can be no important or instructive relevance in this fantastical peregrination, with what Jesus actually taught or with the declared aim of reinforcing belief in the divine origin of his teaching. This demonstrates how far down the by-road of imaginative irrelevance the wagon of new ornamentation has sometimes trundled.

If one examines the records of the life and teaching of Jesus carefully, there is no mention of him trying to develop a new religion; he states quite clearly that he is fulfilling the law, the Jewish law, neither abolishing it nor changing it: he was just ridding the law of obfuscating or even inaccurate scribal interpretation, misleading embellishment in other words. This is not even reformulation. Just as enormous quantities of interpretation and additional material have been fashioned to smother 'Christianity', so the Jewish faith had been, in effect, hidden under a blanket of interpretation by the scribes, ancient and modern. Jesus was purifying, refining the faith with the powerful breath of his teaching, which blew away distracting ornamentation. He was restoring the Jewish faith to its pristine, intended condition. The significant difference, after removing the accretion of centuries of pernickety bureaucratic interpretation, was a change of emphasis, from narrow-minded threatening demands to open-minded loving reassurance on the part of our God, from backward-looking atonement, which was basically negative, to a positive forward-looking philanthropy on the part of all humankind, generated by determined goodwill toward everyone, even when one hates what particular people believe and do.

A very useful example of how decorative thinking began to smother the simple teaching of Jesus is provided by the writer of John. We may deduce, with some certainty, that, as was made clear by the general tenor of the accounts, Jesus taught so as to be understood by ordinary people; his appeal was to them rather than to those steeped in the wisdom of scribal experts in the law. However, the thinking in John is wonderfully deep. The *Daily Telegraph* for Saturday 5th November, 2022, gave John 6:51 as the text for the day: "I am the living bread which has come down from heaven; if anyone eats some of this bread he will live on into the coming age; and this bread which I am going to give for the life of the world is my body." One accepts that the writer went on to say that the listeners began at once to dispute the meaning of what Jesus had just said: "How on earth can this (silly) man give us his flesh to eat?" This retort is just what one might expect, so this particular occasion could have some sort of basis in an actual event. Nonetheless, there is a very noticeable quantity of such almost exasperatingly incomprehensible material in John, and this is difficult to reconcile with Jesus's appeal to 'common people'. We gather that the disciples of Jesus were quite uneducated and not endowed with the learning that the teaching of Jesus, as portrayed in John, would obviously require. Jesus is very unlikely to have spent much of his time addressing such erudite people; it was ordinary people who were his concern. As is suggested in note 8 and appendix 4, the writer of John seems to have been challenged by the abstruse and almost incomprehensible thinking of Heraclitus; the prolonged exploration of such works seems to have affected the way in which he thought: we see this in all the exegesis and preaching attributed by him to Jesus. All writers are influenced by what they have learned during their lives. We should read their works with this principle in mind.

If one assesses what the different writers have said from this angle, one may begin to understand how their thinking and writing have been affected by their lifetime experiences. When we try to interpret what we read in the Bible, we need to make proper allowance for this and we then might be able to see more clearly what Jesus really meant. The basic thinking of Jesus is simple and does not need a learned scholar to explain it, as if it would otherwise be incomprehensible. Jesus's teaching was meant to be understood by almost anyone; when one allows to the stories in John the credibility that the manner of telling seems to support and then treats the teaching and exegesis as the product of the scholarly mindset of a writer, we have a far better chance of profiting from what we read. The Jesus of the Gospels taught us that we should use every possible occasion to try to help our neighbours, that we should use all our possessions, whether material or mental or spiritual, to enrich the world around us, and that goodwill should be used in every dealing in which we engage: hostility, aggression and violence should never be allowed into the proceedings. We make ourselves happy by surrounding ourselves with people we have made happy.

A particular mindset, in which many of these

decorations have been fashioned, is exemplified by an entry in Eerdman's 'Dictionary of the Bible' (Michigan, 2000, p. 702 top right), where it declares (Professor E.P. Sanders, contributor) that Jesus's ministry lasted less than a year, which would appear, if the evidential data are properly examined, to be wrong: the ministry is more likely to have included two Passovers and ended with a third. There is a later claim in this entry that accepting John's account of a longer ministry leaves more questions unanswered than are answered by positing a ministry that lasted a *few months*. **It is the truth with which one should be concerned rather more than the number of questions that may or may not appear to be answered by a proposed solution**. It would not seem likely that the effects of Jesus's teaching could have been brought about in a relatively few months, while the style and content of the events recorded in John are clearly based on convincing evidence from a witness. Postulating a longer ministry of as much as two and a quarter years, perhaps, answers questions that matter, it is suggested, rather better than a shorter one, and makes a more compelling account possible, while assuming a ministry of just a few months would appear to fail to do this adequately. Another indication of flawed thinking is the idea that because *three* Passovers were mentioned in John the ministry lasted *three* years, when any reasonable calculation will recognise at once that the ministry might have lasted very little more than two years.

Examples of decoration may be on show in the different accounts of the crucifixion, the disappearance of Jesus's body on the Sunday – or before – and what is described as his resurrection. Only one account is likely to be right. Comparing these crucifixion and resurrection records in the four canonical Gospels can be illuminating. There is agreement that Jesus was crucified with two others who were criminals, but it would appear that the details offered by the synoptic writers have not been gleaned from a witness in the same way as the details in John seem to have been: there will have been, almost certainly, no fully adult male supporters of Jesus at the crucifixion; there was only the very young son of Zebedee, John. All the rest had, as Jesus foretold, 'run away', apart from this boy John, whose youth, charm and easy familiarity with the High Priest's entourage, will have rendered him confidently safe from any recrimination.

Mark's version seems to be the original of the three Synoptic Gospels, with more elaborate developments in Matthew and some fanciful additions in Luke. When the rich Joseph of Arimathea has had the body of Jesus placed in his new tomb, Matthew has an elaborate sealing of it, followed by an earthquake and an angelic presence whose face was likened to lightning, in clothing as white as snow, appearing to the two Marys and then rolling away the stone from the tomb. Much of this seems to be the stuff of which dreams are made rather than the convincing matter-of-fact reality we find in John's account. Luke's account is less dramatic initially but, with three ladies named later and then a supernatural visitation by two young men, it does not read as if it has come more or less verbatim from a down-to-earth witness. However, the account in John's Gospel is completely natural and rings true: in this, Mary Magdalen (from Magdala), apparently on her own, is the first very early morning visitor to the tomb; her going to tell Peter and John what she had discovered is exactly what one would expect. Even more telling is the subsequent account of the meeting of Jesus with this Mary, when he tells her not to 'touch' him: this is clearly because he would not have been felt by her when she tried to hug him; he was not there in normal bodily form. The explanation given in John's Gospel for Jesus telling her not to touch him is quite without any coherent logic; it has obviously been invented by the writer as an explanation. It is this very failure in understanding on the part of this writer which confirms that the story was almost certainly based on accurate firsthand information from a witness.

The naturally, convincingly sequenced account in John of the discovery of the resurrection is the one that sounds real, rather than the whimsy of a prototype novelist. Particularly eye-catching is the description of the piece of cloth, which had been wrapped round Jesus's head, being rolled up and in a separate place by itself. No doubt there are commentators who will want to argue that this is cunningly plausible invention on the part of the writer. On the other hand, C.S Lewis's assessment of the provenance of these stories in John is far more convincing than the trails of doubt which some sceptical scholars prefer to be seen to pursue.[1] A dispassionate assessment of this account, as well as most of the others in John, almost proves that the source was a very energetic young witness, driven by almost unquenchable curiosity and endowed with a most remarkably retentive memory for both definitive outline and extensive detail. Just as there was Jesus, the ideal agent for God, there was the young John, bursting with youthful energy, the ideal witness of how Jesus was directed by God.

We seem to have a hear-say narrative in Mark, which is then taken and developed by Matthew and, after that, by Luke who reproduces it with a different set of additions. There was an underlying reality, but the writers, lacking firsthand knowledge of the actual elements, provide accounts which demonstrate how their minds worked and how they fashioned material to fill in the gaps for which they had found no reliable information.

ONE

—

There is – or used to be – a coda to many a story: "That's the Gospel truth." Often the teller wanted the hearer to believe what was being told, even though he or she did not completely believe in it: there had been a wonderfully embroidered tale which the speaker wanted to be 'taken as read'. If we examine the Gospels, especially those according to Matthew and Luke, and then 'Acts of the Apostles', critically enough, we may be able to discover what these words may often have in fact signified: we are being treated to higher, as well as more enthralling truths. Many of the accounts present a wonderful introduction to how we might, or perhaps should, feel about what Jesus taught and did, but the details in these images do not remain convincing the moment one starts looking for trustworthy evidence, or tries to find other supporting data.

Many people are deterred by what appear to them to be unlikely claims in religious creeds. However, if, as has been suggested elsewhere, while examining the origins of what came to be called 'Christianity', the more strident improbabilities found in the New Testament are transferred to *higher status,* the realm of the desired and traditional, but improbable in the eyes of some, or even seemingly impossible, while the remainder is explained satisfactorily, what is acceptable as truth, the real Gospel Truth, is more likely to be ferreted out and appreciated. We need claims that are based on more than just wishful thinking, or ingenious imagination, or alluring scenarios, or mind-stretching visions, however beguiling or long-established the stories or visions may be. This is particularly pertinent when the visions or ideas, however plausible they might seem, are those *of only one person;* there may be many, indeed *very* many, who have come to believe in the validity of one particular vision, or a set of visions or ideas, but, without corroborating evidence or supporting witness from an independent source, ideas and visions lack reassuring substance. The existence of an enormous number of believers does not establish that what is believed is firm fact. Some of us feel we need robust, coherent evidence, if we are to believe claims safely and surely, especially when the claims are very important. The claims about

Jesus, both before and after the crucifixion, may seem particularly challenging but nearly every one of them is explicable.[2]

We may be sure, because of the quantity and variety of evidential data, that someone called Jesus, the declared son of Joseph, actually existed and was crucified for sorcery (healing and telepathic powers, including exorcism) as well as leading Israel astray (false teaching, a capital offence in the Torah), as was recorded of someone in what may have been the Hasmonean period (140-63 BC), named Yeshu (Jesus) in the Babylonian Talmud – he was hung (crucified) at a Passover[3] – and in the works of historians who were writing not long after the events, as well as in the New Testament. A very widespread tradition of his teaching lives on after him, although we cannot be sure that we know *exactly* what he taught, because different people have presented different pictures, usually suiting the culture prevailing at the time and in the area of the interpreting presenter, as well as suiting the writer or speaker's own particular viewpoint.

Nevertheless, we may be more certain of the existence and crucifixion of Jesus than we may be sure that Julius Caesar invaded Britain in 55 and 54 BC; Caesar's lucid annual commentaries on the progress of his war in Gaul were, really, propaganda, intended to promote a favourable reputation in Rome – he did not want to be assassinated – for when he would be returning in January 49 BC after his proconsular duties in Cisalpine and Transalpine Gaul had ended. This did not work too well, as we find him writing next about the ensuing civil war, in which his most notable former officer, Labienus, possibly a former protegé of Pompey, fought against him.[4] We may arrive at a better understanding of what life at the top was like in those days if we realise that Caesar was really fighting for his life: at that time, in Rome, the effective motto for some top politicians and generals was "Win and kill, or be killed!" Caesar, in spite of being at least partially responsible for the deaths of a number of opponents – perhaps he was lenient with a few too many – managed to postpone his assassination for only a little over five years. His chosen successor, Octavian (later to be called 'Augustus'), survived, as he had, with the support of the other members of the Second Triumvirate, Antony and Lepidus, perhaps two thousand 'nobiles' (members of families which could boast consuls, for the most part) proscribed and killed, so very few embittered enemies with threatening power were left alive. This is the violent background to the Roman scene which Jesus entered in one of the more remote parts of that extensive empire, when Tiberius, the embittered successor to Augustus, was the emperor.

One should note that a religious development in North America was based on claims that visions had enabled Joseph Smith to 'see' special records, 'written' on *gold* plates. The claims and witness of *only one* man attracted a significant following then, and there are millions of followers still. Furthermore, an examination of Mormon beliefs might find that some of the claims made for these beliefs do not present a persuasive picture of Jesus's family and teaching which suits everyone in our different and supposedly more enlightened era. Any set of beliefs that claims Jesus's life and teaching as its base should fit logical assessments of the records in all major respects, particularly in being applicable to every period in time. It is better when good evidential data support claims: a statement on its own does not often constitute sufficient evidence for its veracity; there should be other identifiable factors which may be seen as satisfactorily corroborating any claims made.

There are so many different faiths, in the present world, demanding credence, that we need to establish sound criteria by which to judge their claims. This is more than a matter of personal taste: it is a matter of spiritual good health. Anyone who states otherwise has failed to address the situation adequately and has not realised that spiritual health may often have some effect on physical health, while good spiritual health is likely to weaken any tendency to depression. This book is an attempt to find well-reasoned arguments which show a way to developing good spiritual health.

The Jews followed a rule that two witnesses (at least) were required to establish something as acceptably true; one witness was insufficient. When we examine the Gospels, we can compare their claims with other relevant evidential data, and look to see whether internal factors, such as convincing coherence and circumstantial detail, provide additional support. If it becomes clear that there is a convincing amount of evidential data to substantiate important parts of particular accounts, we have much firmer footings on which to build any religious beliefs. We should try to discover what there is on which we may definitely rely and whether it might be appropriate to relegate other material to unproven status. What we believe matters, so it should have solid foundations, in just the same way as we need firm ground to hold up our feet when we walk anywhere. If blind unbelief is sure to err, blind belief will be just as likely to lead to error. It might be that there are faiths which lack a sufficiently convincing basis in witness or other evidential data, which also fail to display internal coherence and clear applicability to every region, race and era, and so do not merit all the trust placed in them. If there are to be found characteristics in a faith which tie it to just one area, or suit one race or set of races better than others, or seem fixed in the culture of a particular era or region, or can be expressed best and most effectively in only one language, there should be pause for thought. If it is discovered that a faith's creed or scripture contains dubious claims that appear to be aimed at undermining the basis of other and different faiths, one should approach that faith with even more circumspection.

Faith, it has been argued, is important, especially if it is meant to be universal, so it is wise to know, as has been said, why one should hold to any faith and observe any requirements which that faith appears to impose on its adherents. Belief demanded with imperious claims that it is the only true faith, without any supporting evidence, seems not too desperately different from the highwayman demanding, "Your money or your life!" This is, curiously, not too dissimilar to the end of the Book of Revelation (22:18-19) where the writer declares, without any further explanation, that anyone who adds or subtracts to what he has declared in the book will suffer heavenly punishment accordingly. This claim is supported by no evidence whatever and so lacks convincing authority.

For example, an all-compassionate, all-merciful God will not create something so as to consign that created object to eternal punishment; such a God will not threaten or destroy; such a God will not expect any members of his fallible creation to believe that their own judgement is infallible, nor St Peter's, nor St Paul's nor even the Pope's, or that any particular one of them is here to execute what are imagined, almost certainly erroneously, to be commands from God to punish another, let alone kill that other; no error-prone human being, we may deduce, is here to impose restrictive regulations at God's express command.

Indeed, on p.183 of his commentary on the Gospel of Mark (Tyndale New Testament Commentaries, I-V, p. 1989) the Revd Canon Dr Alan Cole remarks about the Pharisees "…that what they teach depends entirely on human, not divine, authority." A truly based faith in God, which claims to be universal, should have *arguably* divine, rather than just human authority; it should be coherent, equally applicable in every region, in every age, in every society, to every sort of person, of whatever race, and intelligible in every language to more or less every level of mental ability and suit the idea that a creator God will love his creation and want to help it rather than destroy any of it.

While we try to establish what the foundations of any faith might be, we could remember the words attributed to St Thomas Aquinas: "Nihil in intellectu quod non prius fuerit in sensu." This might be translated as meaning: 'Nothing can be understood and mentally organised except insofar as it (in its entirety) has been already experienced by the senses' and then analysed so that inferences, inductions and deductions may be made (see Appendix 3). Of course there is a difficulty: he also believed in higher knowledge, which might somehow be thought to transcend anything which sensory experience seems to substantiate. This book is based on the proposition that God 'is happy' for us to arrive at some sort of understanding of him and how we should live, through working that out from what we read in the Bible and experience in our lives, while we keep this Thomist principle, referred to above, in mind; any higher knowledge will come after everything else has been established and put in order.

Examples of how one may pursue fruitful examination of data can be demonstrated in dealing with three events in the life of Jesus, namely the temptation, baptism and cleansing of the Temple. We can be reasonably confident that these three things happened, as they detract from the divine, superhuman aura of perfection with which the writers wanted to surround their image of the man. The tradition that Jesus began his ministry at around thirty years of age, that his family business was dealing with the wooden parts of building, that his presumed father, Joseph, had left the scene probably well before the ministry, the statement in Mark that Jesus was working in the business, all imply that an explanatory 'bridge' is needed to explain why Jesus changed, at a later stage in his life, from working as a probably well rewarded artisan to the totally different world of an unpaid missionary or prophet, preaching a new way of thinking about religious duties. The temptation furnishes this; during his work he will have become acutely aware of his very remarkable endowments, telepathy and healing, and will have developed his almost overpowering concern for the downtrodden among his fellow creatures: he needed time away from the business to think about what he should do with these gifts, so as to help his fellow man, especially women and children. This was the period of the temptation. Then we have the baptism, at the end of this period of temptation, at which moment God takes over directing Jesus. This provides a clear starting point for the ministry.

The cleansing of the Temple, which behaviour will have been attributed to some sort of mental aberration at the time, is even more likely to have occurred than the first two events; it is immediately obvious that what might be likened to a mental breakdown is quite the reverse of anything the writers would have wanted to say of Jesus. We may be sure that this act of cleansing happened. However, it would *not* have been seen as a reason for having someone put to death, as going berserk in this way in the Temple precincts would have been perceived as being due to possession by a demon. Demonic possession was considered a relatively frequent occurrence, it would seem; this was the province of an exorcist or expert in trepanning rather than that of an executioner. One is reminded of the occasion when a beneficent Victorian visitor to a lunatic asylum was told by an inmate that charity covered a multitude of sins. The visitor agreed. The inmate then went on to say, "But insanity covers them all!" This is more or less true now, and it was true then. All this suggests that the act of cleansing would have occurred fairly early on in the ministry. We see from this that the traditional chronology of these events, as adopted by the Synoptic Gospels, is probably inaccurate. The writer of John's Gospel would seem to have the right chronology. Interestingly, the writer of John makes no mention of the temptation, so, according to the implications of his account, provided the temptation happened, as it almost certainly did, it will have been before the baptism.

TWO

—

The pitfalls of traditional thinking are illustrated by a fairly widespread assumption that, when Jesus was carrying his cross, before he was reportedly relieved of the burden by Simon of Cyrene, he was carrying the upright part as well as the transom (transverse beam); the upright part is likely to have been fixed in the ground beforehand. One might consider, also, details that obviously conflict with common sense, such as shepherds *watching* over their flocks *at night,* when they could not have seen much, and sitting in fields (rather than lying across entrances to walled sheepfolds, when ones with lockable doors – see John 10:1-5 – were not available) as well as looking after their flocks all day. From where were the ideas of the massacre of the innocents and period of exile in Egypt derived? Prophecies from the Old Testament, which do not fit very well, and wonderful imaginations, do not necessarily provide sound evidence for working out what happened during the life of Jesus.

Indeed, Matthew's Gospel contains many difficulties. His enthusiasm for quoting Old Testament prophecies may have induced him to use Hosea's (11:1) 'from out of Egypt I have called my son', although we find, when we have read on further, that this does not fit Jesus or his family at all; he then used Jeremiah's (31:15) 'Rachel weeping for her children', which she was doing in Ramah; Rachel may have been buried in the area but her weeping did not happen in Bethlehem. To add to the difficulties for Matthew, the children 'who were no more' (massacred?) are to return within their own borders (Jeremiah 31:17) which they would not be able to do if they were dead. Matthew's fashioning the story of Herod massacring twenty or thirty babies in Bethlehem seems to have been based on shaky foundations. The absence of any record of a massacre does not mean it is untrue but that absence does not suggest it is true either. Crucially, there is no attested reason for the massacre being enterprised because the idea that Herod had been warned that a future king would be born in Bethlehem, where Jesus was probably not born anyway, sounds very improbable. The difficulties become greater as, with Matthew's chronology, Jesus would have been born in 6 BC, to allow for the two years spent in Egypt and Herod's death in 4 BC.

Another instance of a pitfall was developed from the mistranslation of a Hebrew word in the Septuagint (Greek version of the Old Testament). Instead of 'a young marriageable girl' it had 'virgin'. A better translation of the passage from Isaiah 7:14 is to be found on p. 61 of the commentary of Brevard Childs on Isaiah ('Isaiah', Westminster John Knox Press, Louisville, Kentucky, 2001) '...therefore the Lord himself will give you a sign: a *maiden* is with child and she will bear a son, and will call his name Immanuel', which, as a name, is unique in the Old Testament and is explained as meaning 'God (is) with us'. It is repeated, but not as a name, in 8:10, where it appears in the Oxford Study Bible as 'God is with us.' Isaiah does not provide incontrovertible support for the belief in a virgin-birth and immaculate conception, though the prophecy fits very well, otherwise, with the coming of Jesus. Indeed, translating the Hebrew word *almah* as *maiden* rather than *virgin*, as Childs does, suits those who want to think that Mary was with child before the actual marriage ceremony.

A completely fresh approach is needed, without the accompanying heavy and extensive traditional luggage of often irrational beliefs, which seem to have been developed from almost nothing and with little restraint, or been added without appropriate recourse to factual evidence or sufficient reason; one is reminded of the decision of the then Pope, Pius XII, to issue ex cathedra, in 1950, the dogma that the 'Virgin' Mary had not died a normal death but had been assumed, body *and soul*, into heaven as if heaven is a locatable place and the soul material in the same way as is the body. A Mrs F…, who lived in North Oxford then, could not believe this arguably baseless dogma – on the grounds that there was no clear supporting evidence – and was excommunicated as a result: a most unholy outcome.

The natural inclination to venerate his mother should not be allowed to eclipse the purpose of Jesus's ministry. Nor should the elemental importance of Jesus and his teaching be allowed to distract us: it is God with whom we are primarily concerned. We should bear in mind that the signposts and communication system that indicate where and how we might discover him and be connected, however important, are secondary to God. A signpost to Oxford is not the city nor is the road: in this instance it is Oxford that matters most. Jesus is immeasurably more than just a sign – he is more like a totally reliable satnav – while the Holy Spirit is much more than an inanimate road, but these two, all the same, are secondary to God, even though we cannot know anything about God except what we learn from or through these two.

Another example of traditional theological thinking, flawed by assumption and preconception, is provided by Professor (John) Marsh in his commentary on the Gospel of John (Penguin, 1968) in which he wonders (p. 657) why Luke puts his somewhat melodramatic account of the 'miraculous' catch of fish near the start of Jesus's ministry while John puts it at the end of his Gospel with the 'third' – it was actually the fourth in his account – appearance of Jesus after the crucifixion. He seems to have missed the fact that Luke's account is clearly exaggerated, as well as misplaced as to the detail of the fishing practice in use then, and likely to have been gathered from a more distant source than that in John. Luke's understanding of the chronology seems weak. John's account sounds as if it comes from a firsthand witness,[5] whereas that in Luke sounds as if it has come through several 'hands' and then been embellished. The different accounts of the events in the life and ministry of Jesus, as presented in the four Gospels, are not equally reliable as to what they claim.

Yet another mistaken notion seems to be the idea that Jesus was serious nearly all the time because his message was so important: no laughter and few smiles. It becomes clear, if one looks at the material dispassionately, that Jesus had a wonderful sense of humour, as was pointed out by James Cary, a BBC sitcom-writer, in chapter 7 of his book, 'The sacred Art of Joking' (SPCK Press, 2019 – p. 78, for example). Anyhow, it is difficult to imagine a charismatic leader who inspired the level of loyalty which Jesus aroused being without a sense of humour.

An early example of flawed thinking is provided by none other than Paul in his first letter to the

Corinthians 11:3-15. Somewhat in the manner and style of the Qur'an it seems tied to the period in which it was conceived and written. How could one imagine Jesus teaching this?[6] Where does Paul, incidentally, demonstrate wit or humour in his letters?

The reliability of the evidential data that underly what individual Gospel writers say matters far more than appears to have been understood by many commentators. Much more attention needs to be paid to assessing the reliability of original sources before their claims are accepted as valid, and a great part of this can be achieved just by analysing the likelihood and coherence of what the writers actually say. A prominent sign that care is needed is the calculation that Matthew and Luke used a source consisting, for the most part, of sayings of Jesus. When one hears the word 'sayings', the idea of 'Chinese Whispers' inevitably comes to mind: the accounts of the original events may have been changed, to a greater or lesser extent, and possibly acquired additions, before they came to be written down. The exceptions to this caveat may be the parables: their style and construction do not invite much change or embellishment that might mislead.

If one examines the Gospels carefully, one may chance upon a number of instances where a lack of logical coherence demonstrates conscientious recording by the writer of what he had heard and, thereby, the fact that there was a tradition which he was trying faithfully to preserve; the errors more or less prove that there was an original underlying truth, whose exposition the writer had, understandably, got wrong on account of the inaccuracies in the memories of the people who had made up the chain along which the stories had arrived in the writer's hands.

A slightly more curious example is provided by Luke in 11:41 where he had misinterpreted a word and written 'alms', when the word concerned would have had more to do with cleanliness. We find ourselves following the converse of Polonius's advice to Reynaldo in Hamlet II.i.66, "By indirections find directions out": we find our directions from the Gospel writers' mistakes or indirections, just as many teachers understand their pupils better from what they get wrong than from what they get right.

Some hymns present quite impossibly silly pictures of Bethlehem in what we now call late December: "In the bleak mid-winter/ Frosty wind made moan,/ Earth stood hard as iron,/ Water like a stone,/ Snow had fallen, snow on snow ...' for example; the 25th December is early winter, not mid-winter, snow must be rare in Bethlehem, while penetrating frost might seem almost impossible; the idea of large quantities of snow lying on ground deeply penetrated by long-lasting frost, so early in winter and in the eastern part of the Mediterranean, seems outlandish. Lovely words by Christina Rossetti, with entrancing music by Gustav

Holst, do not always tell helpful truth. In fact, they must do damage, so implausible are the claims which people are expected, *unquestioningly*, to accept; their mental detachment from reality weakens real commitment to the meaning, and so purpose, of the ritual. Sadly, there are many other hymns, almost inexplicably popular, of which the words are even sillier. On the other hand, "It came upon a midnight clear" is a far better hymn, even if the time and implied date are wrong. It is true that the idea of angels playing golden harps and singing would seem to belong to the realm of higher truths, but the ideas of peace and goodwill on earth are exactly what Jesus's ministry was about.

There is another factor which distorts adequate thinking: misleading tradition. Just as Jesus taught us to give up being enslaved by the stultifying detail in the scribal interpretation of the law, we need to stop being slaves to foolish traditions, such as the very potent idea, inherited from Judaism, of atonement for sins. The well-known word 'scapegoat' is a glaring exemplar of this tradition. This is a negative approach, not a positive one. In about 1961, on a visit to Balliol College, Oxford, seeing the lush late-September lawns, I asked the gardener what weed-killer he used. He replied that he did not use weed-killer, he used fertiliser: he made the grass grow so well that the weeds did not have a chance. We should make our own good deeds grow so well that sin does not have a chance. It is positive good that wipes out negative sin much more effectively than anything else. Teachers who spend more time praising what is good than censuring what is bad, are more likely to succeed. Perhaps we should think more of doing good in the future rather than thinking, often vainly, of trying to atone for sins in the past, however much we may, and indeed should, try to express our regret. Jesus showed us how love for one's fellow man is the strongest driver for good, for making the world a better place, for building God's kingdom.

After all, *metanoia*, which has been misleadingly translated as meaning *repentance* rather than *changing one's mind* – and so behaviour – introduces another example of a wrong-headed tradition which needs correction: it is the good deeds of the future that matter, with a **new mindset**, far more than the misdeeds of the past, committed with the old mindset. Change is far more important than repentance. Indeed, if those correctly found guilty by the due process of the Law and sentenced to custodial conditions had to do good deeds by way of atonement, especially if they had to help those whom they had wronged, real reform of the prisoner would be a far more likely outcome and prison numbers would, as a result, be reduced; if prisoners had well-prepared positive action plans in their minds, as well as firm provision for housing and occupation, arising from activities prior to release, their future would be brighter in the world outside prison. Everyone would profit.

One might note here that the nonsense of human rights is another area where a change of mind is essential: it is our *responsibility* to look after our neighbours which is of primary importance, the *rights* (a neutral concept) of our neighbours, whatever they might be, are not what need the greater attention; it is our *inherent obligations,* a positive concept, to our neighbours and their needs which matter more. We should change the way we look at matters such as these. The resulting conduct would then be better than it is at the moment, when only the rights of other people are being taken into account.

One could add, as an aside, that Marsh noted a very important point (p. 658 in his commentary on John's 21st chapter): just as Jesus had returned to God, after being crucified, Peter might have been thinking that they, the fisherfolk, should then return to fishing. It seems strange that Marsh appears not to have seen that this very point makes it very likely that the source of what is in this Gospel is firsthand. However, Marsh may have implicitly recognised, subconsciously perhaps, the primacy of the information in John, even if he appears not to have recognised this in so many words.

When we start examining the Gospels, our enquiring minds should be *tabulae rasae*, with no assumptions or preconceptions, so that we may impartially evaluate the evidence. In any review, we should abide by, it is suggested, a salutary guiding principle: God has no need of miracles, even if many of us may cling to them;

indeed, for some it seems to be an essential crutch for keeping their faith upright amid all the encircling challenges.

Another crutch that a few people seem to require is the idea that every word in the Bible is the inalienable, unalterable, as well as inspired word of God, when it has often been translated (many words in a language do not have satisfactory equivalents in other languages) sometimes mistranslated, sometimes misheard during dictation with, often, the eventual written part being the result of a chain of accounts taken from oral tradition, etc. It is just as vital to remember that it was compiled by witnesses and writers who were anchored in their own times and often wrote to promote their own idea of God and the importance of their own people. On top of this, there are occasions when accounts diverge from previous accounts in the Bible or where contradictory statements are made or when extra details seem to have been added in unconvincing fashion. The Bible has been written, translated and handed on by humans and absolutely no human is infallible, so no one can logically or wisely believe that every word in the Bible is the unalterable, unmistaken and unmistakable word of God (see note 6).

Particularly interesting are those occasions in the Gospels when someone who is ill is described by Jesus as asleep (in a coma) but thought by others, and the writer of that Gospel, to be dead. Even now, in spite of all the technical advantages we enjoy, people continue to be consigned to mortuaries when still alive; it is likely to have been a much more frequent occurrence then, and Jesus's telepathic powers will have known that the apparently dead 'patient' was not actually dead but in a coma.[7] Whenever the miraculous is introduced into an account our suspicions should be aroused. The factual parts of John's Gospel contain nothing that cannot be explained in material terms, apart from, perhaps, the disappearance of Jesus's crucified body, even if the telepathic and healing powers attributable to Jesus appear so great that 'miraculous' seems to be the only suitable epithet. Furthermore, Paul, in his letters, mentions no miracles, nor wonderful interventions as recorded in Acts, even though one might have expected him to have heard of some miracles from Simon Peter, whom he knew, if there had been any particularly notable ones. Had there been convincing substance in such accounts, Paul would almost certainly have related at least one supernatural intervention, as chronicled later on in Acts or in the Gospels.

The nearest thing to a miracle Paul tells us of, apart from how he himself was converted, is the appearance of Jesus to his brother James – from whom Paul will have learnt this at firsthand – after the crucifixion, in 1 Corinthians 15:7. Jesus, unlike other ghosts, was attached to people rather than places. It will have been this appearance of Jesus to him that changed James from being an unbelieving sceptic into a believer in the divine basis of Jesus's teaching. The letter attributed to him displays the wisdom and command one would expect from the brother of Jesus who will have felt the guiding hand of Jesus while he 'wrote'. God's direction of Jesus and his providing Jesus with scriptural quotations may seem miraculous, but equivalent occasions of inspiration may be found elsewhere. God may use Jesus, via the Holy Spirit, to communicate with us even now.

One should remember that Paul, although he seems never to have smiled, was totally convinced that the source of the teaching of laughter-loving Jesus was divine, while the writings attributed to Paul demonstrate clearly that he was completely sane, highly intelligent, erudite, but with his 'feet firmly on the ground'. He was neither easily misled nor deluded. It is only the foolish and bigoted who would rashly dismiss Paul's testimony as the unfounded *fantasies* of a dreaming visionary. His contribution to the cause of Jesus is not only vast, but extremely securely based. He is one of the most important blocks of masonry in the fabric of the Church. The Church may be made up of people, but the people who are the building blocks need to be held together so as to make the structure of the Church firm. It is the beliefs which spring from the teaching of Jesus through the writings of the New Testament, where Paul is so prominent, which are the cementing mortar of the 'building'.

The information provided by the Gospels, Acts of the Apostles, New Testament letters and early Church historians, as well as the entry in the Babylonian Talmud, provide what amounts to clear evidence that Jesus's teaching was sufficiently successful and revolutionary to be perceived as a threat to the priestly authorities, while much of the evidential data would seem to point to the teaching as coming from God; it did not come from visions, nor is there only one source for the claims made. What amounts to the truth is there, clearly to be seen, and is reassuringly firm. No crutches are necessary for the progress of trust in God to be safe and confident. Indeed, Alan Cole, on p. 134 of his commentary on Mark, writes, "God does not always meet our needs by *supernatural* [my italics] miracles: that is the exception, not the rule." There is also the concomitant consideration that we might expect God to disguise any element of the miraculous in such a way that it would often be difficult for anyone to discover it.

One should add here that the Greeks must have been right when they posited that any idea of a supreme being should be without any recognisably anthropomorphic characteristics. Xenophanes had noted that, as Ethiopians had gods who resembled Ethiopians, horses, if they were to decide that there were gods, would think of them as looking like horses; cows would have gods that looked like cows. Xenophanes, who is described as the first philosopher to be a theologian, by Anthony

Kenny in his very useful 'A Brief History of Western Philosophy' (Blackwell, 1998), is credited by him with declaring that the supreme being was neither finite nor infinite, neither changeable nor unchanging, such characteristics being anthropomorphic and relevant in this world but not necessarily elsewhere. A little later, Heraclitus, a philosopher who flourished in Ephesus about five hundred years before Jesus was crucified, called his idea of a supreme being 'LOGOS', and declared that this being was responsible for everything which exists, both of which ideas occur as fundamental points at the beginning of the Gospel of John. This makes it clear that the writer of the Gospel was steeped in the philosophical outlook of Heraclitus, who too had lived in Ephesus five hundred years earlier.[8]

One cannot rationally attribute to God, these Greeks had implicitly realised, the idea of anthropomorphic purpose or the possibility of his encountering any challenging difficulty – this latter would be a contradiction in terms – as one cannot know anything about what is outside the bounds of our finite earthly experience. They had worked out that such a being must have existed but not that there was a loving relationship between that being and his creation. It was Jesus who was needed to reveal that essential belief in God as a loving creator father; this is the *euangelion* or gospel. We may work out that there is a supreme being and that somehow our existence and all our resulting perceptions are due to him, but we can hardly do much more than that on our own. As an example, the doctrine of the Trinity is anthropomorphic in much of its concept, and so not really logically tenable in the form in which it appears in the Nicene Creed: any attempt to define what is, by definition, indefinable, is illogical: we are not equipped to define God. All we can do is believe that Jesus was directed by God and that God communicates with us, when we are able to manage to listen with the help of prayer, by the Holy Spirit. Deducing that we are all made in the image of God is thus meaningless, as we can have no idea of what our supposed image has been derived from. Declaring with certainty that there is a bodily resurrection, to introduce the dead into the 'next world', is similarly impossible to substantiate. In the same fashion, imagining that Jesus is or was the actual son of God in any way that is markedly different from us all being children of God is not logical. It is the soul which pilots the body, and it is that which might, in some way, be divine.

Interestingly, Jesus was said to allude in John 10:34 to the quotation in Psalm 82, v.6, which declares that all Jewish sons are children of God. All we can do is calculate from the available evidence that Jesus was nearer to being God's representative on earth than anyone else, before or since, and that during his ministry he was directed by God in a way that no one else has ever been directed. We are not in any position to say, for instance, that Jesus was pursuing a path ordained by God: we cannot know anything about God; any commentator making such a statement is seriously damaging any possible claims to theological understanding on his part. However, as God's appointed agent from the moment of baptism, we may think of Jesus as God's anointed in a metaphorical way, thus possibly validating the general idea of Jesus as messiah – 'christ' in Greek – as it means 'anointed', but not as the imagined vengeful, all-destructive force which the Jewish mind and writings foretold of the anointed one to come, who would destroy all adversarial powers and rescue the world from utter moral and political chaos, instating the Jews as rightful 'top nation'. One might think of chapter 13 in Mark's Gospel. Those who want to think of Jesus as 'messiah' may have to resort to the anointing by Mary of his feet in John 12:3, although Jesus says it is for his burial. Jesus's ministry was about loving behaviour which saved, not vengeance that destroyed.

The anti-Jewish stance in the early 'Christian' tradition will have grown out of a complicated background. The imperial power of the Romans seemed to require circumspection in what one 'published' and an effort to try to find favour with them, if the chance arose. However, it was the priestly Jewish authorities in the High Priest's entourage who were responsible for persuading the Romans to have

Jesus crucified, not the general Jewish populace. These authorities continued their efforts to extinguish the legacy of Jesus after the crucifixion, according to what we learn about Paul in Acts and from his letters. It is very clear that the downtrodden Jewish 'masses', whom Jesus so courageously championed, would not have been responsible for the terrible execution of Jesus. Any hymn that describes the mass of ordinary Jews as hating Jesus is not supported by adequate evidence and is, in reality, a disgraceful and damaging libel. As a result, the clear fact that Jesus never renounced Judaism nor Judaic law, has not, one may argue, been acknowledged widely and openly enough. What we, quite possibly mistakenly, call 'Christianity' is, rather, a new Judaism. Some Jews may not be keen to accept that those who believe that Jesus's teaching was from God are 'new' Jews, but it is new Jews that 'Christians' claim, in effect, to be.

The concept of 'messiah', or one divinely anointed to save Israel, is purely Jewish and relevant, really, only to Jews, as is suggested in the Old Testament. We should probably rethink some of the conceptual basis of our belief system. We should also try to persuade the Jews that we are part of the prophecy in Isaiah 2:2-5 & 11:1-9 where all the nations of the earth are envisaged as streaming to God's holy mountain (compare Revelation 7:9)[9] and so acknowledging the God of the Jews as their God too: "They will neither harm nor destroy on all my holy mountain, for the earth will be full of the knowledge of the Lord, as the waters cover (and fill the bed of) the sea."

We might, at the same time, point out the pertinence of the prophecy in 53:9 which, translated from the Hebrew, says: "And they made his grave among the (plural) wicked [among = between the two crucified on either side of Jesus] and with the (singular) rich [the tomb of the rich Joseph of Arimathea] in his deaths." As emphasised in the note, the Delphic imprecision in the prophecy makes it almost certain that this is a divinely inspired prophecy of enormous significance, while the otherwise very surprising distinction of plural, in the original Hebrew, for the wicked and singular for the rich, noted by Alec Motyer in his 'The Prophecy of Isaiah' (IVP Academic, 1993, p. 435)[10] makes the prophecy even more apposite. Combined with the earlier prophecies in the second and eleventh chapters of Isaiah, this makes, arguably, the most important combination of prophecies anywhere. It is Jesus who is to be the spring from which the river of peace-making knowledge of the Lord will flow. All the divinely inspired springs, the later prophets and visionaries, may be thought of as vital tributaries to this river of faith in the one true God.

Similarly, we can be pretty sure that Jesus reappeared to a special group of Jewish people, in some form, not always easily recognisable and of an insubstantial variety, after his death on the cross. But any idea of eternal life in some sort of heaven is beyond anything we might calculate, as Jesus seems to have made clear when he was reported as saying that in heaven people neither marry nor are given in marriage. This divinely inspired explanation comes in Mark 12:25 and is copied by Matthew in 22:30 and Luke 20:35, who both clearly thought this an important point. The idea that any mortal being would be bodily resurrected in or into heaven is anthropomorphic and beyond the bounds of common sense, as heaven is unearthly, non-spatial and 'beyond' anything we could rationally try to define. Similarly, trying to imagine life after death is likely to be a waste of time (see appendix 3). It is suggested that reputable teachers of religion should not be encouraging anyone to engage in such speculation. It is taking good care of *this* world, with the help of God, which should be our concern, not bothering about the unimaginable and totally indefinable next.

One should remember too, that our creator God, according to what Jesus taught, is a loving father. Such a father does not consign his beloved creation to eternal fires after bringing 'his own' into the world. Anyway, the idea of hell, for the Jews, had been developed from the rubbish dump, Gehenna, in the valley of Hinnom, where continual, if not continuous, fire, consumed much of the refuse. Apt this would seem to be for those whose lives had not served more use than rubbish;

but then, what for people such as Vladimir Putin, whose egotistical stupidity, fuelled by deluded advisers, including the Patriarch Kirill of the Russian Orthodox Church, inflicted such torment, murder, pillage and rape in Ukraine and, as a result of the ill-judged invasion, deprivation on nearly everyone in the world? What about the support given to Russia's invasion of Ukraine by the satanic leaders of the regime in Iran? We must deduce that God loves even them, even if God does not love what they have done.

We cannot possibly tell what lies ahead after this life, so we should not waste any time trying to work that out. All we may suppose, perhaps, is that hell could be the hair-raising clarity with which we might see what we *should* have done in our lives, when we failed to do it, and what we *should not* have done when we failed to check ourselves from doing it. The writer of Ecclesiastes may have said in 12:12, 'One further warning, my son: there is no end to the writing of books and much study is wearisome', but in v. 14 he wrote, 'For God will bring everything we do to judgement, every secret, whether good or bad.' The judge is not identified; we may find that *we* are the judges, judging ourselves, with every detail inescapably clear.

One could add that having ringing in one's ears the claimed promise, that belief in the divinity of Jesus is the only thing that matters and that it guarantees eternal life, has nothing directly to do with how one should live. A desire for eternal life is a purely selfish object in life. Martin Luther had realised that the aims of his contemporary religious authorities then were, in effect, directed at selfish ends only. Dr Michael Banner in 'Christian Ethics' (Wiley-Blackwell, 2009) puts the matter thus (p. 60): '...how could one achieve a perfect love for God and neighbour, when the pursuit of those works was for the sake of one's own salvation? ... How can one be selfless for the sake of the self?' The commentating decorators have missed the evident fact that Jesus's ministry was about deeds that helped his fellows and they have failed properly to take into consideration the very pertinent New Testament letter of James where (2:14) we have, 'What good is it, my friends, for someone to say he has faith when his actions do nothing to show it?...(v.17) So with faith: if it does not lead to action it is by itself a futile thing.' James is making it clear that faith without works is an empty faith.

Such is the wisdom that wells up in every line of the letter that it is difficult to reject the tradition that it comes from the mind of the probably illiterate brother of Jesus, though, just as probably, written down later by a writer steeped in Hellenistic culture and tradition, with some written evidence to help him, or with prompting from carefully preserved oral tradition. There is wise authority permeating the letter and this is unlikely to have come from the mind of James, son of Zebedee, who was executed as early as 44 AD, which was before people had begun writing anything down. Augustine would appear to have been right in his attribution; and, as this James was executed in AD 62, by which time Paul had probably written most of the letters he is credited with, attributing to him the ideas set out in a letter seems defensible.

Particularly interesting is the tenor of the letter which suggests that the idea that faith is so important that works do not matter is unjustifiable: faith without works is not true faith. Might he be trying to correct an impression developed in some minds from the teaching and letters of Paul? Might this be evidence of some sort of rift between the first leader of the Church and Paul? In his letter to the Galatians, when Paul writes about his staying with Peter in 1:18-19 so as to get to know him, he writes only of seeing James without any further comment. Interestingly, Peter was based in Jerusalem at this moment so he was 'junior' to the Church's first leader, James, and Paul was spending a fortnight with Peter rather than with James: did he already know James well or was there some other reason?

A final caution might be found in Banner's explanation of why Martin Luther became a monk: *to escape hell*. How can any sane person believe that a God of love has created 'hell', a place of eternal torment, for those whom he has created who fail and who do not adequately repent and atone for their failures? How can it be thought that a God of love would create anything so as subsequently to consign that creation to eternal torment?

THREE

—

When one decides to study the origin and purpose of the Gospels, the first task is to look at what they say and how they say it. One has then to try to calculate where their information may have come from and so how reliable it may be. After that, one has to try to work out what changes the writers may have made, adding, subtracting or making even more radical alterations, and then why they may have made these changes. The questions why, what and how need to be addressed before one accepts anything that is said at face value. Deciding whether the Gospels are meant to be biographical or factual is secondary. The categories were made to classify what people had already written; the writers of the Gospels did not write so as to fit any specific category. The environment in which the Gospels were composed and the reasons for them being written in the first place, should also be considered, before one tries to categorise them as being, for instance, biographical or concerned with the study of history. If one can decide why, with what evidence, how, and when they were written, one is in a stronger position to categorise them. To try to categorise them before doing this may be a waste of scholarly energy, as one should know first exactly what one is trying to categorise. Anyway, what matters far more is whether there is any likely truth in them and what that truth might be and must mean. When looking for that truth, one should exclude every previous assumption. Also important is whether the writers managed to achieve what they intended in the context of the time when they were writing. After that we should try to establish if what they say might be relevant now, to what extent and how.

One might recall that there is a claim in the Gospel of John that the writer has written it so that the readers might believe in the divine truth of the message of Jesus. It is a religious tract, perhaps, in this respect; the other three Gospels might be adjudged to be little different in character and ultimate purpose. The purpose in the minds of the writers will have influenced the *way* in which they said it as well as *what* they said. They believed that their message was absolutely true and of vital importance to the whole world.

One notices that the first canonical Gospels were written three decades or so after the crucifixion of Jesus, while that of John seems to have been written almost another two decades after them. It would seem reasonable to assume that nothing was written down straightaway, as it did not occur to anyone that doing so might be useful or necessary: Jesus was expected to return so soon that such an effort would have had no chance of providing any benefit to anyone. However, Jesus did not return as soon as expected. They had not thought of the idea that Jesus returns to each of us when we die. Those who believed in the divinity of Jesus's message will have begun to feel concerned that, with the 'passing' of those who had been original witnesses to Jesus's ministry, memories of great importance were being lost. They will have felt that some record should be made to save at least some of these vital memories. Hearing of the loss of Peter, possibly crucified (upside-down?) in Rome in about 65 AD, is likely to have been an electrifying shock to them all. To rectify the situation someone seems to have decided to have the Gospel of Mark written down.

The 'Mark' we know of as having been connected with the spreading of the message of Jesus, although the name Mark was a common one at the time, was 'John Mark' (Acts 12:25), who had accompanied Paul and was said, by an early bishop, Papias, to have accompanied Peter as his 'interpreter' or 'explainer', a sort of personal assistant; there is another mention of this Mark in the first letter of Peter 5:13. The actual statement of Papias declares that John the Elder, the most probable writer of the Gospel of John, said that Mark recorded accurately, though not in order, what he remembered (by implication from Peter's teaching and preaching) trying to leave nothing out while including nothing false. John the Elder will not have known Jesus nor will he have known John Mark, so he will have acquired his knowledge of the correct chronology from a witness (John the son of Zebedee, very probably) and possibly other witnesses. It is the knowledge acquired from witnesses that will have enabled John the Elder to pronounce authoritatively on the matter of chronology, as well as accuracy, in Mark's Gospel. This John Mark will, very probably, have known the *lingua franca*, Koine Greek, better than Peter, whose mother tongue was Aramaic; coming from a well-to-do family, he may well have been able to read and, it is suggested, write as well, unless he used the services of scribes.

Following on from the lack of order cited as appertaining to the chronology in Mark, it should be borne in mind that Matthew and Luke are repeating what they have learned from Mark, which does not amount to confirmation that something is true, in spite of the Bellman's claim in Lewis Carroll's 'The Hunting of the Snark' that what he said thrice was so. There is less reason to doubt the chronology in John, as it was, in fact, arranged by the same person who was credited with casting aspersions on the chronology of Mark. The authority with which he writes is so lofty that there should be few who would dare cast doubt on it. Commentators might do better when they recognise this fact.

At this point one might consider a number of points in conjunction with the foregoing. Mark is almost certainly the first of the canonical Gospels to have been written. The name links it with the John Mark of whom we are told something in Acts 12 and elsewhere, and in some letters attributed to Paul. We learn from Acts that he was the son of a Mary who owned a sizeable house and had a maid, and that he was a cousin of Barnabas. We then note that there are, in this Gospel, one or two accounts that contain details that strongly suggest first-hand witness input, such as the interjection, near the end of the Transfiguration (Mark 9:5-6), that they might construct three shelters, one for Elijah, one for Moses and one for Jesus, *for he* (Peter) *did not know what to say.* This will not have been literary artifice on the part of the writer: it will be a true record of the event; this could come only from Peter.

Again we have, when the apparently dead young girl is resuscitated out of her coma, an instruction that she should be given something to eat (Mark 5:43), which again suggests firsthand witness. She was also described as being about twelve years old, the age, plus one day, at which a girl became an adult, which is further circumstantial detail. Jesus's command to Peter in Mark 8:33, 'Get thee behind me, Satan!', is unlikely to have been invented by the writer: it very probably had eyewitness testimony behind it, while Peter, who loved and worshipped Jesus, is the most likely source. The otherwise inappropriate, and hopelessly incompetent, assault on the High Priest's agent would not have been invented by the writer: it must have been provided by a witness and Peter, although he almost certainly did not name the assailant, avoiding both shame and criminal blame, is the likely one. The witness to John's Gospel had known the victim personally and so was able to name him. A very important point here is that Jesus is reported as saying, though not by Mark, "Sheathe your sword!" Jesus was not to survive by the sword nor was Jesus's teaching to be spread by the sword, nor enforced by it. " 'Vengeance is mine, [mine alone, *not* any mortal's] I will repay' says the Lord" (Paul's letter to the Romans 12:19). Paul goes on to say that one should treat one's enemy well, not punish him, let alone kill him; all those who still kill people now or killed people in the past in the name of God, actually kill with the inspiration of Satan. Such teaching from Paul is clearly inspired by God.

The three times denial of knowing Jesus, on the part of Peter, is not the stuff of invention either. Of particular interest is the unique statement in Mark that the cockcrow was a 'double' event (although there is a suggestion that the trumpet-signal at three o'clock was threefold); here it should be noted that Jesus's prophecy is that Peter will deny he knows Jesus three times before the cock crows twice, and that the *first* cockcrow is not mentioned in Mark's account of the denials, only the second; it might be that the idea of the cock crowing twice was of a double signal of the time rather than an actual cock crowing on two different, possibly well-separated, occasions or that there was an earlier cockcrow signal at midnight which, obviously, would not have been mentioned. Peter would probably have remembered his claim that he would never deny Jesus at the first cockcrow, had there been one. This might be further evidence of firsthand information and how such information becomes distorted in the process of being handed on. Incidentally, a double signal is 'echoed' in some church clock chimes in Southern France which toll the hour twice with a noticeable time gap between each set of strikes (true in 1990).

There is a cautionary point: there are very interesting details about Peter in the Gospel of John which are not found in Mark, such as the washing of the feet and Peter's interchanges with Jesus, and the time when Peter asked the witness to the Fourth Gospel, John, who was going to betray Jesus; these surely would have been mentioned if the writer had learned about them. Most revealing, however, is the omission by Mark of how Simon came to be surnamed Peter. At the start he is named 'Simon' and is not called Peter until Mark gives the list of disciples without an adequate explanation there as to why the name has come to be changed. If there had not been a number of people making up the chain of informants behind Mark's version, rather than just one, or, at the most two, these important details are unlikely to have been lost. However, it is true, as Mark was compiled from unordered papers, that some of the 'pages' may have been lost, such as those which chronicled the very last days after the crucifixion. Pages covering these events may have existed before they were lost. All the same, we may be sure, even if Mark's was the first Gospel to be written, that the firsthand witness behind John's gives it primacy in trustworthiness as to details of events, sayings and chronology, although not as to preaching or any exegesis of that preaching.

Professor William Barclay, in the second edition of his commentary on Mark (Edinburgh, 1956, p. xix, §iv), notes other details that suggest eye-witness material as the source. The tradition that Peter's teaching lies behind this Gospel seems well-founded. Another example of eye-witness input is provided by the account of the lady whose haemorrhage was healed when she touched the four-tasselled hem of Jesus's cloak. The fact that Jesus felt 'power going out from himself' would not, indeed could not, have been dreamt up by the writer; then the coup de grace from the accompanying disciples: "You can see the crowd of people pressing up against you and yet you ask 'Who touched me?'" This is live reporting, coming from the ineradicable memories of a disciple, presumably Peter. The same incident is reported in Matthew but some details are omitted, showing that his account is dependent on that in Mark. The detectable losses and changes in Matthew and Luke from what is in the Marcan account would seem to support the thesis that Peter gave the original information while he was preaching or conversing with the first recipient of that information, whose unordered records were then later used by the writer and editors of the material. Mark's is credited with being the first Gospel, and it appears to be based on information gathered from Peter. The genesis of Mark's Gospel is in stark contrast to that of the Gospel of John, which seems to have come from a wonderful witness straight to the writer (who knew Mark's Gospel and very probably the other two as well), although many years after the events. All this suggests strongly that the first Gospel may be connected with the John Mark of whom we know something.

It might be helpful for some readers if one is reminded that the first three Gospels are often described as synoptic, or sufficiently alike as to content and arrangement as to be to considered comparable, as 'see-able' and seeing together. Although, originally, Matthew was considered to be the first to have been written down, with the Gospel of Mark coming after both Matthew and Luke as merely a condensed summary of the two, it has since become clear that the writers of Matthew and Luke were, almost certainly, copying Mark and then incorporating new information which they had learned, often indirectly, probably, from the survivors of the time of Jesus's ministry. This will be the 'source' entitled 'Q' or 'Sayings of Jesus.'

However, the lack of reliable knowledge of chronology and local geography suggest that Mark's Gospel is quite possibly third hand: John Mark may have made notes on sheets of papyrus and these used, by whoever wrote the Gospel of Mark, to produce the Gospel itself. The writer of the notes will have known the relatively simple details of what Jesus taught quite well; it is the accompanying details of the circumstances in which the various examples of teaching occurred which the 'interpreter' will have needed for his 'explanations', if and when these were asked for or considered appropriate. The lack of knowledge of the chronological order of events in the Gospel supports the argument that it was constructed from an unordered collection of 'papers'. The sheets covering the last days of the story were either lost or never existed, so the contrived ending is quite different in style from what went before. The Gospel may well have been written in Rome and not Palestine, as the knowledge displayed of Palestinian customs and geography in the Gospel is weak.

A lack of chronology is demonstrated in the Synoptic

Gospels, when the cleansing of the Temple is placed late in Jesus's ministry, so as to be seen as the main reason for the authorities wanting Jesus eliminated. Being in the power of a demon, or being, in other words, out of one's mind, as has been said already, was not a good enough reason for having someone crucified; but it was a good reason for Jesus's family wanting to take him out of public life, as reported in Mark 3:21 & 31. Indeed, it might be argued that claiming to be messiah was not a death-meriting offence either, just as being a prophet was also acceptable. Undermining the authority of the religious teaching (dogma) was, however, a capital offence, which is the reason given in the Babylonian Talmud, as has already been explained (see note 3). The raising of Lazarus, which the Synoptic writers seem not to have learned about,[11] so strengthened the fame and influence of Jesus that he was perceived as being a very serious threat to the authority of the High priest and the members of the Sanhedrin, as is related in the Gospel of John. Indeed, the size of the crowds gathered on Palm Sunday suggests a very strong crowd-pulling event, which hearing of the raising of Lazarus would have been.

The lack of a true grasp of the order of events in the Synoptic Gospels is shown clearly by the absence of any reference to a significant number of Jesus's visits to Jerusalem, which Jesus, as a conscientious Jew, almost certainly will have made so as to attend those major festivals which, though not obligatory for residents of Nazareth, were obligatory for those who lived sufficiently near Jerusalem. The Synoptic Gospels also miss the fact that the feeding of the five thousand occurred at the time of the Passover. Even stronger is the idea, which comes in Mark 3, that the family of Jesus wanted to take him out of public life on the implausible grounds that attracting massed crowds was to be taken as a sign he was out of his mind; on the other hand, cleansing the Temple *would* be taken as a clear sign of mental disorder. Another discrepancy is the placing of the 'Temptation', presuming that it occurred, after the baptism; it is more likely, as was pointed out at the end of the introduction, to have happened before God took over directing Jesus at the baptism; indeed, the fact that the Temptation is neither mentioned nor any time allowed for in the Gospel of John suggests that the Synoptic writers were probably wrong to place it where they have, as was also argued in the introduction.

The priority of Mark's Gospel is supported by developments in the other two Synoptics of what is reported in Mark. Of particular interest are developments that would appear to heighten Jesus's affinity with God. In Mark 10:17-18, when the young man asks Jesus, "Good teacher, what should I do to be allotted eternal life?", Jesus's reply starts with "Why do you call *me* 'good'? No one is good except the one (and only) God."– no doctrine of the Trinity here, as

Jesus clearly implies that he is neither God nor equal to God. But Matthew, when he deals with what seems to be the same incident, has Jesus (the word 'good' has been transferred to the deed and not applied to Jesus) responding "Why do you ask me *about* the Good? There is (only) one who is good." Here, in this rather wooden reply, which does not quite fit, Jesus does not specifically differentiate himself from God. The curious addition of Jesus asking 'Why do you call me good?' makes it clear that this was an indelible memory in the mind of the witness behind Mark's Gospel, thus attesting to its reliability at this point. Interestingly, Luke, in 18:18, keeps to the original wording because, one might guess, he could see how Matthew's account did not fit together very well.

Again, in Mark 6:3, Jesus is described as a 'joiner-builder', possibly the most important worker but probably not the only one, in the family business, but in Matthew 13:55 this is changed into 'joiner-builder's son' so as to distance Jesus from such mundane pursuits. Not only does this suggest that Mark's version is prior to Matthew's but also that the desire to establish Jesus as completely equal with God, promoting the idea of the 'Trinity', may have been growing out of fertile wishful thinking and not from down-to-earth information. One might note here that there is no mention of the 'virgin birth' in Mark. It would seem most unlikely that Mark would have failed to mention this if it had been part of the accepted canon when the Gospel was written. This provides further evidence for the priority of Mark.

The clearest indication that Jesus is not God is given by the one writer, John, who wanted to suggest that Jesus was really God in human guise. In chapter 12:44-50 Jesus is described as saying, "Whoever believes in me *does not so much believe in me, but rather in him who sent me; to experience me is to experience him who sent me.*" Then, later, "I do not pass judgement … there is a judge … the word I have spoken will be the judge on the last day. *I have not spoken on my own authority but the Father who sent me has himself commanded me what to say and what to preach…I say just as the Father has instructed me.*" John is making it absolutely clear here that Jesus is *not* God but is acting for God under his direct instructions at the time in question. Paul in his first letter to the Corinthians, 11:3, where he is so hidebound that he displays almost antediluvian incomprehension, writes, "But I wish you to understand that while every man has Christ for his head, a woman's head is man, as Christ's head is God." If two are co-equal, neither is the head of the other. Paul follows with a list of instructions about how men and women should dress their hair, which is reminiscent of the rules and regulations once imposed in Iran by the morality police on the luckless ladies there.

Paul clearly implies that Jesus, the visible representation of God, had been following directions, and was not God's equal. A coda to this is the fact that Jesus was often described as praying; even in John, 11:41, Jesus gives thanks to the Father for hearing him. God cannot be thought of as *praying*, let alone to himself. Jesus was not God, however closely directed by him. The Council of Nicaea was tied to its era, misguided by Constantine and did not reach logically tenable resolutions. Arius demonstrated that he understood matters somewhat better, and was then treated badly for doing so. Ian Wilson, in 'Jesus: the Evidence' (Book Club Associates, 1984, p. 180) gives further examples of unholy outcomes in the Vatican: one concerning the divinity of Jesus – Arius was right, and not the Vatican – and the other, unsurprisingly, papal infallibility which no conceivable form of logic could possibly ratify. On the day quoted (15th December, 1979), Edward Schillebeekx, because he had suggested, both properly and, as it happens, correctly, that the nature of the divinity invested in Jesus at Nicaea had *perhaps* been overstressed, found himself summoned to face trial before the same body that had condemned Galileo for saying that the earth went round the sun, in 1633. On the same day, in another room, the career of Hans Kung was ended because he had questioned the idea of papal infallibility. Foolish claims formulated in the realms of unreason should have no place in any modern theology – certainly not if that theology hopes to be considered worthy of any respect.

The tendency to alter details to fit the desired interpretation is well-exemplified at the beginning of Mark's Gospel, where the original prophecy in Isaiah has the voice announcing that it is the straight way which is to be in the wilderness (remote unpopulated area), whereas Mark has the voice, rather than the straight way, in the wilderness, so as to suggest that John the Baptist, who *is* in the wilderness, is the very voice which prophesies in Isaiah. Both Matthew, supposedly a Jew who might have known the Scripture better, and Luke, copy Mark in making this error. One is tempted to think of the 'straight way' as being the 'clear way': 'Love your neighbour, even when you do not love the deeds of this neighbour, whom God has created, to show your love for God.' The wilderness is a loveless, pathless world into which Jesus has come to preach the dominion of the straight ways of God's love.

There is a very revealing absence of general agreement between the two accounts of the birth of Jesus and childhood provided by Matthew and Luke, as well as a lack of any evidence to support what they claim. This makes it very likely that their accounts are no more than calculations from those prophecies in the Old Testament which they thought pertinent. We saw exactly that when Matthew claimed that not entirely appropriate prophecies, which he had found in Hosea, must refer to Jesus and his parents. This area of speculation is all excellently covered by Geza Vermes in 'The Nativity' (Penguin, 2006).

When we hear or read the Gospels, we need a benchmark by which to judge the trustworthiness of the statements made in them, the extent of the underlying truth. As has been argued elsewhere, the factual accounts in the Gospel of John provide excellent criteria by which to assess what we may encounter in book, talk or preaching. The fact that the witness, who furnished the stories, provided no parables is of little consequence. The parables are so widely applicable, so obviously intelligible with only a little help, so timeless in their relevance, that they demonstrate perfect congruence with the aura left by Jesus; we may put our trust in them as having their origins in the God-directed teaching from Jesus, almost without question. Again, it is the unintended meanings that confirm the internal truths to be found in them. A very good example is the parable of the 'Sheep and the Goats' (Matthew 25:31-46), which is echoed in Leigh Hunt's 'Abou ben Adhem':

> Abou Ben Adhem (may his tribe increase!)
> Awoke one night from a deep dream of peace,
> And saw, within the moonlight in his room,
> Making it rich, and like a lily in bloom,
> An angel writing in a book of gold:—
> Exceeding peace had made Ben Adhem bold,

And to the presence in the room he said,
"What writest thou?"—The vision raised its head,
And with a look made of all sweet accord,
Answered, "The names of those who love the Lord."
"And is mine one?" said Abou. "Nay, not so,"
Replied the angel. Abou spoke more low,
But cheerly still; and said, "I pray thee, then,
Write me as one that loves his fellow men."

The angel wrote, and vanished. The next night
It came again with a great awakening light,
And showed the names whom love of God had blest,
And lo! Ben Adhem's name led all the rest.

This very valuable parable tells us that we show our love for Jesus and for God in the way in which we treat others. What we do shows what we believe; even the self-declared atheist, whose purposed ignorance may seem to some to scar the scene, fulfils the will of God when lovingly looking after 'neighbours'; it is the self-absorbed, self-promoting atheist who troubles little about his fellowman, and may even betray contempt for *imagined* inferiors, who might be in some difficulty. I once did some voluntary work with adults who had learning difficulties: it was clear to me at once that there was no way in which I was superior to them; I was different, I was trying to serve, but I was not and did not feel superior. In a curious way, the goodwill that appeared to permeate the whole enterprise seemed superior to anything I had encountered before; it was as if they were superior to me.

Another valuable parable is the one of the Talents, in the same chapter, vv. 14-29 (cf parable of the ten minas in Luke 19:11-27, from a different occasion), which tells us that whatever we have, whether material or in personal endowments, should be 'used' for the benefit of others: all our so-termed 'possessions', knowledge and abilities are, in reality, responsibilities; what matters is how we use them to help others.

However, the parable that expresses even more eloquently than that of the 'Sheep and the Goats', how one behaves as a true servant of God, is that of the 'Good Samaritan', predictably found in Luke, the master of story-telling, 10:29-37. Another of Luke's masterpieces (15:11-end) is the parable of the 'Prodigal Son' where full repentance, on the part of the younger son, and complete forgiveness, on the part of the father, bring all-pervading loving peace, which only the failure completely to forgive, on the part of the elder son, mars in any way.

Being the first Gospel to be written down seems to provide some assurance that the material in it is more reliable than that in those which come later, when there are disagreements. It is thought, as has been pointed out already, that the Gospel of Mark came first because much of it is found in Matthew and Luke, and that the pattern of repetition fits the idea that Mark was first rather than a condensed copy of the other two, while developments of one or two accounts in Mark suggest that Matthew and Luke are adapting an existing tradition so as to fit the ideas behind their presentations better. Indeed, if Mark was copying why did he omit all the accounts of genealogy and birth? It might be argued that the failure of Matthew and Luke to agree on much of what they related concerning Jesus's birth and childhood might have given Mark pause, but that would seem less likely. Even better, the idea that the Gospel was based on reports of acts and sayings of Jesus seems to be borne out, to some extent, by the occasional detail that must almost certainly have come from an eyewitness, with Peter fitting that 'bill' better than anyone else.

The last Gospel to have been written, although John Robinson argues against this in his book about redating the Gospels ('Redating the New Testament', SCM Press, 1976), is almost certainly that of John. The theology in it is not only idiosyncratic, as if coming from a mind steeped in Greek Philosophy, but very sophisticated, not early. Much more importantly, the vivid narration attests almost indisputably to an eyewitness with a remarkable memory for detail. The fact that so much was written so much later than the first three Gospels implies an eyewitness who was very young at the time of the ministry of Jesus and whose illiteracy resulted in nothing being actually written down until an enthusiastic writer found the witness many years after the ministry of Jesus. Initially youth, and later modesty, meant that this supremely valuable source did not press the importance of what he knew on others: he was the reverse, as has been pointed out already, of a thunderous, ambitious, self-promoting lad, as jestingly portrayed by Jesus when he nicknamed him and his brother Boanerges. However, his capacity to remember detail was as remarkable as the ability of Homer, even if the bard was reminded of the right words by the accompanying music so as to 'remember' every word in those twenty-seven thousand lines of Iliad and Odyssey.

The Gospels were written by people who were convinced of the divinity of Jesus and his teaching, the first three using what they had learned from second-hand sources, at best, and often more distant than that. The exception is the Gospel of John, which seems to have been written with firsthand witness material in it, while some of it, if not most, even seems to have been written down during question-and-answer sessions: the presence of the witness is implied in John 19:35, where the flow of blood and water from Jesus's side, after being pierced by the soldier's lance, is being attested by someone else who is actually there as a witness; again, in 21:24, where the present tense of the participle, 'witnessing' rather than 'witnessed' or 'has witnessed', suggests the actual presence of the witness while these final verses are being written down. Another correction comes in 4:44 & 45 which suggests that the witness is there to help; remembering the account in the Synoptics about this visit to Galilee, the writer repeats the account of a prophet being without honour in his own country, but is then corrected by the witness who will have explained that the people there, contrary to what he says he has just written, were very pleased to welcome him because of the 'miraculous' deeds of his of which they had recently heard. The witness was, almost certainly, illiterate, so the writer will have often been telling the witness what he was writing while he was doing it.

The body of teaching, as exemplified in the parables, together with the aura of Jesus we find in the Gospel of John, display such authenticity that we cannot doubt the conviction and sincerity of the writers. This is a case in which the 'prosecution' has to find powerful contrary evidence, which atheists, such as Professor Richard Dawkins, have failed, so far, adequately to do. There were many who believed Jesus was God's special envoy and were prepared to endure persecution and even death for their beliefs. Some of these had known Jesus personally and witnessed his 'reappearances' after the crucifixion. The argument that they would not have willingly died for what they did not have strong grounds to believe to be true provides such powerful support for their claims that doubt seems foolish, particularly when there were so many who died for that faith.

The Gospel writers may present the parables and more complicated matters for our consideration, but we do not seem to learn from them a great deal about the law which Jesus had come to fulfil. We have accounts of some exchanges with the religious authorities but not of what Jesus said to ordinary people. However, it is not desperately difficult to calculate the sort of things which he might have said, and said very often. He was adjudged guilty of false teaching. The authority of the scribes, Pharisees and the High Priest with his entourage depended on successfully enforcing the rigid and seemingly endless, often almost pointless, detail in the interpretation of Judaic law. Jesus is very likely to have explained, very frequently, exactly how and where all this detail in the interpretation of the law was an ass. It is likely that he made clear the simple principle that it is by loving our neighbours that we demonstrate love for the one-and-only God; but we seem not to learn much more than that. This teaching, about what the law was really meant to be, is what will have made Jesus extremely unpopular with the religious authorities, but will, at the same time, have made him extremely popular with the ordinary people; it will have attracted their interest and enthusiastic support.

With regards to the Gospel of John, the writing down of the witness's memories of Jesus, at the express wish of the writer, might be likened to Peisistratus, tyrant of Athens in the late 6th century BC, keeping the blind bard of the Iliad and Odyssey hostage – Homeros, which is not a name, means hostage or surety – until he had recited all his priceless memories to an army of scribes. As has been argued in two earlier books, the factual statements, as opposed to the teaching and exegetical material in John, should be trusted and these provide benchmarks by which to calculate the reliability of what the writers of the Synoptic Gospels claim.

FOUR

—

To start with Mark, in our search for what may be considered reliable outside John, seems appropriate. He gives no genealogy, echoing the stricture to be found in the letter to Timothy, probably spuriously claimed to be from Paul, which suggests that occupation with genealogies and stories which lack evidence is to be discouraged, while the Revd Canon Dr Alan Cole, in his commentary on Mark, gives an interesting picture of how Jesus should be understood (p. 105): not only Saviour, but also "*God's appointed agent on earth.*" It might be worth noting another development at this point. 'Satan', in the earlier parts of the Old Testament, meant an adversary, while 'diabolos', from which our word 'devil' derives, meant one who bears false witness, a slanderer or libeller. These are purely human activities. The devil is our inclination to serve ourselves in ways that go against what we should be doing, if we are trying truly to serve God. We serve God by doing our best to look after his creation, our fellowmen and everything else around us, with goodwill. The devil in any one of us may infect others; the devil in Hitler infected millions. A telling example of what and how the 'devil' works was provided by what a boy said of his twin brother when they were aged perhaps four: "I do try so hard to do God's will, but Francis does tempt me so." That twin brother became a very effective and widely loved priest.

We may remember that the name Jesus is the same as that of Joshua who presided over the fall of the walls of Jericho. Those walls might be thought of as representing the barriers to access to God because of the rigid application of a Byzantine array of religious regulations. Perhaps we may think the barriers against others, who are not Jews, reaching God are also being pulled down.

We inherit, however, as has been said already, a salutary comment on Mark from Papias, an early bishop, who, quoting John the Elder, said that what Mark recorded was free of embellishment, but not necessarily in the right order. The frequent lack of explanation for events in his account, and of chronological markers, – except euthus (immediately on again) in very early chapters – would seem to bear this out. John's Gospel is quite the opposite in this respect. An early example is Mark's account of the recruitment of the first disciples, which is not all true to life and very wooden, while fishing was more of a late night activity than a daytime one.

The account in John seems much more likely to have come from an eyewitness, as each event there develops naturally from the preceding one. Indeed, it becomes clear almost at once that Mark not only lacked access to firsthand evidence but also, unless it was a later 'redactor' moving the punctuation, adjusted his account to what he believed to be right, as we have, as has been pointed out already, the incorrect idea that Isaiah was prophesying that the *prophet* would be in the wilderness when it was the *straight way* which was actually going to be in the lonely place. Then we are given a picture of John being dressed and fed in a way which is associated with Elijah, although in the description of Elijah in 2 Kings 1:8 the hairiness attributed to the prophet may have been more like the hairiness of Esau than the hairiness of his attire. We have further exaggeration with the claim that everyone from the neighbouring region and from Jerusalem was coming to John to be baptised in the Jordan: to say 'very many' would have been more plausible. It is true that the quotation of God sending his messenger before his coming is correctly applied and comes from the start of chapter 3 in Malachi. As an aside, when we learn that John baptises only with water, while Jesus will baptise with what we call now the 'Holy Spirit', we might do better translating this as 'Breath of God': breath is life: baptism is about being able to start a new spiritual life.

A point of interest, noted by commentators, is the preservation of Aramaic words in Mark's text. Peter's 'interpreter' will have noticed these particularly, as mementoes of his early life, and will therefore have retained them in his notes. The writer of the Gospel, noticing how their aura was so different from that of everything else, may have reproduced them so as to endow his account with authenticity; these Aramaisms, indeed, do exactly that.

The Gospel of Mark starts with the title: '(The) beginning of the Gospel of Jesus Christ'... This is, in effect, a claim that Jesus, as God's anointed, is the bringer of good news. It may be argued that the good news was twofold. It was both that God loved every single one of us, however bad or evil the deeds, and then that the kingdom in which the love of God would rule in everyone's hearts was being heralded, together with the new understanding that God 'always forgives', although we will still need God's help to forgive ourselves when we realise how we have performed in this life: the picture of atonement presented then, and still presented, must surely be seriously misleading.

Hitherto, the God of the Jews had usually been pictured as a God to be appeased and sacrificed to, hedged about by implacable labyrinthine laws of which any infringement was adjudged to be sin which then had to be atoned for. The first part of the good news was that Jesus had come to free the Jews from these enslaving manacles of the law; the second part was that God is a God of love, a loving father, rather than a God of vengeance, and that this love would turn the world into heaven on earth. One outweighed past sins (atonement) far more effectively with future acts of kindness and care. The painful part of the new regime was the abandonment of the old culture (metanoia). It might seem easy to forgo the tribulation imposed by a previous culture but this is not necessarily so; some Russians, around 1990, when Gorbachev was in power, did not like the absence of authoritarian government; they had become so accustomed to tyranny that they preferred what they were used to. Many Jews preferred the tyranny of the law: it may have been intricately pernickety in the extreme, but it was supposed to be definite; this was even when the law appeared impenetrable and required a bureaucratic genius to find out exactly where and how it was definite…and then produce an incomprehensible explanation as to how that might be.

The account of the baptism was almost certainly not gathered from a witness directly: the claims of supernatural accompanying signs may seem appropriate, but God does not need such extravagant extras to show that it is from him that a message comes, while the thesis that Jesus underwent temptation, or testing, *after* his initiation, rather than *before*, makes little sense: with the baptism, Jesus, as his directed agent, has become the nearest thing to God on earth, so tempting him would seem quite inappropriate. As an aside, one may note that baptism by John was intended to be followed by a change from one's previous life and the taking up of a new life-style to replace the old. This implies that Jesus too might have been undergoing change: beforehand he had been fully human, with the propensity to fail which that entails, but was now becoming a new man, God's agent on earth. He was not God before but, with God's taking over his direction at the baptism, Jesus was becoming God's legate and interpreter; any addition, such as that which a temptation or any other testing might have been expected to confer, was now, one would think, completely unnecessary. There are arguments that support the placing of the temptation, as recounted in the Synoptics, such that Jesus now needed to undergo final preparation for his mission, but the omission of any time, let alone mention, of the temptation itself in the witness-backed account provided in John is too strong to allow much credence to be attached to the Synoptic account of it. Had there been a period during which Jesus had left the scene to reflect, before starting his ministry, the writer of John would have found a way to describe it which would not have damaged in any way his desire to present Jesus as the equivalent to God.

We have a date marker: the imprisonment of John the Baptist, which is followed by the statement that Jesus then began his ministry, preaching in Galilee. This date mark is contradicted, in effect, in John's Gospel, which appears to base much of the early ministry in and around Jerusalem and recounts occasions when the disciples of Jesus discuss matters with those of John, clearly after the first Passover mentioned in John's account. There is also the statement in John 3:23 & 24 that John was baptising and had not yet been thrown into prison. This implies a good many weeks, if not even some months, between the start of Jesus's ministry and the later imprisonment of John the Baptist (see note 11). This is further confirmation of the theory that Mark's Gospel is based on information gathered from Peter, as he will have been earning the family living for much of the first year or so of Jesus's ministry, and so not a witness to most of the early Jerusalem-based period of that ministry. If Mark had obtained witness-based information more widely than from an almost solely Petrine source, he would have covered that part of the ministry, which almost certainly occurred, in and around Jerusalem. We may do well, therefore, to consider John's Gospel, which gives details of a great deal of activity in and around Jerusalem, as vitally important in this respect. The witness for John's Gospel was almost certainly John the son of Zebedee. As this witness was the youngest and indulged one of the family, he had plenty of free time to follow, first John the Baptist and then Jesus, being conveniently based, very probably, in a family-owned house in Jerusalem. However, one should note that the theology in John's Gospel is that of the writer (probably John the Presbyter, as has been said already, to whom the three letters with that name have been attributed), as the witness did not remember any of the parables, let alone teaching, which explains the preparedness of the High Priest and his entourage to tolerate John the witness and deal with him in the delivery of preserved fish from the Zebedee fishing business, even though they will have known of his associating so much with Jesus; but, because he remembered none of the teaching, he was not being corrupted, as far as they could tell. They did not foresee the future, far-reaching, overmastering power of the witnesses's detailed memories of the life and character of Jesus.

There is an important divergence from the Gospels of Matthew and Luke in that there is less detail in Mark of what Jesus actually taught. This is not surprising as this Gospel was composed using almost contemporary accounts of memories of Jesus, which will have contained probably only outlines of the teaching. The teaching was simple and well-known by the 'interpreter' so he will have written down the events which were the context of the teaching rather than extensive details of the teaching itself. It is very clear from the inventive embroidery found in the other two Gospels that the writers will have imaginatively constructed accounts using what they could discover from those who had heard Jesus and were still alive. They will have fashioned what they thought appropriate for those occasions when they wanted to illustrate Jesus's teaching. The likelihood of their accounts coming after Mark's account is demonstrated on the numerous occasions when it is felt by them, as has been argued, that the divinity and authority of Jesus needed to be amplified and emphasised: they built on, sometimes changing, sometimes expanding, what they had 'inherited'.

There seem to be three parts to the theme of Jesus's teaching which appear in Mark's Gospel: 1, think again and change your basic aims (repent); 2, God loves us all (euangelion or Gospel); 3, the kingdom of love (goodwill) on earth, echoing God's love for us, begins construction here and now with Jesus as God's appointed architect (a spiritual, though far more important and immeasurably greater, Christopher Wren). If one adds how unlucky for us that all Christopher Wren's plans, for rebuilding the parts of London destroyed by the Great Fire of 1666 were not implemented, one could add, with far greater regret, how sad the teaching of Jesus has not yet been adopted by all the world. Perhaps the many 'Jews for Jesus' will manage to change the picture. The plans in the parables will demonstrate how we are to show God's love and build God's kingdom. Jesus may be presented, sometimes, as a challenging mystery, but his teaching is for everyone, not just a specially enlightened few to whom alone has been given the ability to understand enigmatic precepts. The teaching of Jesus, as it is for everyone, is simple to understand, even though it may often be less easy for us to follow that teaching in our lives. Professor William Barclay, writes (p. 58 in his commentary), addressing the breaking of Sabbath rules by Jesus's disciples, when they plucked ears of corn and removed the husks before eating them (2:23-28): "Religion does not consist in rules and regulations. ... If a man might become a Christian simply by abstaining from work ... on Sunday, by attending Church, ... saying prayers and reading his Bible, being a Christian would be a very easy thing. Whenever men forget the love [goodwill] and the forgiveness and the service and the mercy that are at the heart of religion and replace them by the performance of rules and regulations religion is in a decline. Christianity has at all times consisted far more in doing things [positive] than in not doing things [negative]." Religion, he explains, is at once both easy (to understand) and difficult to carry out in the normal course of one's life. So it is clear that any religion, when it is used to incite war and invite death, is from the devil and not from God.

FIVE

—

Chapter 1 of Mark begins with the terse claim that Jesus was Messiah (passive adjective, meaning *anointed* for God), that he was the son of God, although this may have been developed by later editors, and that he was presenting an account of how the good news from God began to be preached. We then, at v. 9, have the baptism of Jesus by John, which appears in every Gospel.

As the part which the Baptist is portrayed as playing diminishes rather than adds to the divine status that is regarded as an essential attribute of Jesus, we may be reasonably sure, as was pointed out in the introduction, that its inclusion is correct, a validation of the story, and not there by 'artistic licence': God's special agent does not need any ritual initiation by a lesser mortal.

However, as has been suggested, the accompaniment of the descent of the Spirit in the manner of a dove (v.10) and a heavenly voice (v.11) are more probably extra ideas that were thought necessary additions.

The first event after the baptism, apart from the significant number of days allotted for the temptation (v. 12), was the almost certainly somewhat misplaced account (vv. 16-20) of how the first disciples were recruited (see note 11). It is almost certain that the true account of the recruitment of the first disciples is to be found in John. Indeed, a multiple alert is sounded when we read that Andrew and Simon are fishing by day (v.16) and leave their nets and boats on the spot (v.18), while James and John were mending their nets in their boat (v. 19), which might rock anyway, rather than where there was more space to do it properly, on land. This contradicts the account in John. However, an interesting point is raised: the brothers James and John had a father, Zebedee, whose business was successful enough to have 'hired servants' (v. 20), employees in other words, so their boat might, perhaps, have been larger and not the only one in the business. There is no special reason to add this piece of information, so it is very likely to be right. The first event (v. 21) in Mark's account of the ministry is preaching with authority in the synagogue in Capernaum, about twenty miles Northeast of Nazareth. We may be fairly sure that Jesus taught in synagogues, early in his ministry, as inventing this is not essential to the validation of the message intended by the Gospel writers. The authority (v. 22) with which he taught, although that could be higher truth as opposed to actual truth, fits perfectly with the contention that at the baptism God took over directing Jesus, now his special agent; God's direction, while Jesus taught, will have ensured that all was available in his mind when needed and without error, while, when preaching, he will have had God's unfailing reassurance; this is what will have conferred the air of authority while he performed. The astonishment is to be expected, as Jesus was a 'recently retired' Galilean artisan (joiner-builder), and so would have been stereotyped in the majority of minds as ignorant of anything appertaining to higher studies, such as knowledge of Jewish scriptures and the law.

If we may take the picture presented by the very true-to-life stories in John's Gospel as a guide, although he does not give examples of exorcism, we may be sure that Jesus drove out what were perceived as evil spirits, but not quite so sure that the evil spirits recognised the healing powers of Jesus and also expressed this recognition vocally and loudly. The evil spirit of the man whom Jesus cured (vv. 23-26) was not so much in evidence that attendance at the local synagogue was considered undesirable. It is clear, however, that Jesus's powers of telepathy and exorcism were just about preternatural and so his fame will have spread locally with great rapidity.

We then have Jesus in v. 29 going into the house of

Simon and Andrew and curing Simons (to be called Peter) mother-in-law of a fever. Her then serving them would not have occurred in a strictly run household. This is very likely to have come from eyewitness testimony and emphasises that the circles in which Jesus and his disciples moved were very different from those in which formal religious practice was almost ostentatiously observed. Peter's wife is mentioned when Paul might be writing of his now having a wife too, who is also described as a sister-in-Christ, in I Corinthians 9:5. If he did have a wife, as might seem possible, one hopes he looked after her better than did some other husbands at that time.

With sundown in v. 32, sabbath now over, reading that greater numbers were hoping to be healed makes convincing sense, even though the numbers may have been exaggerated somewhat, as this is supposed, probably incorrectly, to be early during the ministry. The absence of any detail implies that this report is not directly dependent on any witness evidence.

We learn next that Jesus went to a remote spot to pray, long before daybreak, and that the disciples went looking for him and eventually found him. How the writer might have known this is difficult to calculate, but it would seem very possible, if not likely, that Jesus prayed long and earnestly: Jesus was only human and will have felt the need of God's help all the time; one should remember his cry of 'Eloi, Eloi, lama sabachthani?' from the cross!

When the disciples found him (v. 36) Jesus said that he had to preach in other places too. The lack of coordinating detail suggests that this sort of thing may well have been a regular occurrence, but not necessarily at this juncture. There may well have been a need, on the part of Jesus, to replenish the energy that his constant healing may have used. 'Everybody looking for Jesus', so early in the morning, sounds a little exaggerated.

The claim that Jesus preached in the whole of Galilee sounds like an overstatement too; nowhere is any mention made of Sepphoris, the largest town in Galilee at that time.

Then, vv. 40 & following, we have a leper approaching Jesus and begging to be cured. The healing of this leper, who may have had a skin disease that was misleadingly described as leprosy, fits well with Jesus's powers and reputation. 'Leprosy' was a fearful scourge in the days of Jesus, but many varieties of skin discolouration were termed leprous, when they might not have been chronic, and were definitely not true leprosy or, in modern terms, Hansen's disease. Jesus's powers of healing will probably have dealt with the problem of the 'leper' fairly easily, particularly if the root of the problem was psychologically induced eczema. Jesus will have known that any instruction to tell no one would be ignored; the cured patient would certainly tell all his friends, while everyone else in the area would find out anyway. This 'extra' demonstrates Jesus's sense of humour and the authenticity of the account at the same time.

Naaman, the esteemed Syrian general, whose story is recounted in 2 Kings 5:1-14, was demonstrably not suffering from leprosy but some other skin disease, as the chemicals in the Jordan at that time of year had the cleansing properties needed to cure it. Indeed, 'true leprosy' was not yet an established problem in Israel at that date, as it did not appear in that area until around the time of Alexander the Great in the late 4th century BC.

We have a surprising claim in v. 41 that Jesus was moved to anger; this will have been because the sufferer from this so-called leprosy had been excluded so unjustly from all regular human contact. However, the idea that Jesus's fame now spread so rapidly (v. 45) that he could no longer enter towns would seem to be an exaggeration...or was this why he did not enter Sepphoris?

Chapter 2 starts with Jesus 'preaching' in a house, which, by definition, must have been relatively small. The account, had it been obtained firsthand, is likely to have explained whose house it was and even how he came to be there. Indeed, the reported presence of spying scribes in v. 6 makes it clear that Jesus's appearance would have been expected in this house, and so would have been prearranged. However, the details of the roof being dug up in v. 4 so that four men could let a paralysed man on a mat down into a room to be healed by Jesus seems to be based on a true story, even if it *is* third hand.[12] Then we have the rather improbable description of the spying scribes sitting (v. 6) in this overcrowded dwelling. It would seem rather more likely that the scribes learnt of Jesus curing this man, which inevitably implied the forgiveness of sins, *after* the event.

Jesus's telepathic understanding of what people were thinking (v. 7) would have happened so often that including this detail of knowing what was in the minds of his critical hearers in v. 8 is to be expected. Another detail that is difficult to reconcile with a tightly crowded house is the idea in v. 11 of the healed man being able easily to pick up his mat and then walk out. So unusual was the extent of Jesus's power to heal that universal astonishment was inevitable but such crowds make it likely that this event occurred when the ministry had been well established, thus reinforcing the claim that the Synoptic Gospel writers had not had access to accounts of an earlier part of Jesus's ministry which had been based in the Jerusalem area. A highly important point is made (vv. 10–11) when Jesus is reported as saying that, to show his sins have indeed been forgiven, the man should get up and walk. The subsequent amazement (v. 12) on the part of the crowd will have been a frequent occurrence.

Jesus, by curing disease, was, in the eyes of some, acting for God, when only the Temple authorities were supposed to be able to rule in such matters. Disability and illness were considered to be retribution from God for sins that must have been committed and that the only way of 'escape' was ritual atonement as prescribed by the scribal interpretation of the law. This presented problems as it would often have been difficult, if not impossible, to discover exactly what the sins might have been. Jesus was preaching a new Judaism that was designed to end this ridiculous tyranny of the religious authorities. It would seem curious that there will have been many occasions when blatant sins were not visited by subsequent illness or disability and that the authorities failed to account for this.

The chapter continues in v. 13 with Jesus teaching as he walked along; his voice must have been penetratingly clear. We then have the riveting statement in v. 14 that Jesus recruited Levi, assumed to be the Matthew after whom that Gospel seems to have been named, a Jewish tax gatherer. There is no reason given as to why there should be a customs house in this particular spot, so the event would seem to be out of context, demonstrating the lack of chronological order in this Gospel. However, his successful bid to gather the taxes will have been obtained, perhaps, from Herod Antipas, so he will have been working for the 'enemy' *and* profiteering at the expense of ordinary people – one needed to cover the cost of what one had promised at the 'auction' to pay for the bid as well as earn a living. One might wonder if the 'customs house' was a border taxation point for goods being transported between jurisdictions. This 'Levi', or Matthew, is not mentioned by John, but then he may have been a relatively passive, even shadowy follower, whose future importance would lie in his being able to pass on some memories of what Jesus had taught to a writer of the Gospel with his name. It is possible that the source of information about this incident was Peter himself.

Jewish laws of cleanliness forbade eating with unclean people, such as collectors of taxes inescapably were, so excoriation by the rigid-minded law enforcers was more or less guaranteed: they will not have taken into account that, in choosing to follow Jesus, Levi had left his damned and hated trade behind and, since he had changed his mindset, was no longer sinning. Only those who meticulously followed every detail required by the scribal interpretation of Jewish law were without sin in the eyes of the authorities. The people of the land, the common people, who were considered careless of properly observing every scribal stipulation, were sinners whose company was to be eschewed. This information that Jesus associated and ate with such sinners (v. 15), as it adds nothing to the picture which the Gospel writers were keen to present, is almost certainly right. The brilliantly aimed retort (v. 17) that Jesus had come to heal sinners and not the virtuous, makes it clear that this is inspiration from God in the mind of a former artisan.

We now encounter followers of John the Baptist

(v.18), who were said to be fasting then, querying Jesus's disciples' apparent failure to observe fasting rituals.[13] Matthew 11:2-5 has John questioning Jesus's status and authority via his disciples when he is in prison but Luke, apparently copying Matthew, omits reference to John's being in prison when he recounts, with many of the same words, what must be the same episode in 7:18-20, although he adds the embellishment that it was *two* of John's disciples who had been deputed as questioners. The writer of Mark must have thought this important and so wanted to include this piece, but it is clearly without any obviously anchoring context here.

Following on in v. 19 we meet a theme which is faintly echoed in John 3:29-30, about rejoicing while the bridegroom is present, and that the days for fasting will come (v. 20) when the bridegroom has gone. There is no enhancement of Jesus's divine status in this story of John's disciples asking these questions of him, so it is likely to be founded in fact. The absence of this detail in John's Gospel might be noted, as it seems a significant point and one that John would have been interested in had the witness mentioned it. This reminds us that just as Peter probably continued to earn his living, from time to time, the witness too almost certainly continued to supply the High Priest's household with preserved fish from his family business, so he might have been 'away on business' when this happened.

Incongruously, there follow in vv. 21 & 22 the semi-parables of how new and stronger cloth, which has not yet been shrunk by being washed, damages any old and weaker cloth which has been shrunk if it is used to patch that old cloth, and how new wine put into old skins ruins the skins and so wastes the wine. Jesus's teaching was so new and so different from the old established way of looking at and understanding scripture that it required a completely different mindset; the new and the old were almost incompatible, so damage to the old from the new was to be anticipated. The previous and apparently stable ways of religious thinking presented by the scribes and in which the great majority was steeped was under threat. The new teaching was challenging the old.

After this, in v. 23, we have the account of disciples idly plucking ears of corn to eat while they walked, and the question of the correctness of such behaviour on the sabbath, since reaping, threshing and preparing food counted as forms of work forbidden on a sabbath, which might have seemed reasonable to the scribes but not, evidently, to Jesus, as the dictum (v. 27), 'The sabbath was made for man and not man for the sabbath', shows. This contained the further implication that anyone who wanted to help another was right to do this on the sabbath even if the help was classed as forbidden work.

Particularly informative is the statement in the story of the holy bread that it was Abiathar who was High Priest (v. 26) when it was, in fact, according to the account in chapter 21 of the first book of Samuel, Ahimelech. This early apparent mistake may betray a lack of care on the part of the writer or editors of the Gospel, or of later copyists, which cautions the reader against accepting every statement made in the Gospel without question; this might even be taken as a powerful marker to support the reliability of John's writer as compared with that of the other Gospels' writers. However, it is true that both Matthew and Luke avoid saying who the High Priest was, when they copy Mark in their accounts – nor do they say that the sabbath was made for man and not man for the sabbath, which is a failure on their part. When Jesus said that the son of man was lord of the sabbath it could well mean that any man, if the circumstances of caring for the world and one's fellow man required it, could rightly disregard the pernickety restrictions imposed by the scribes in their extravagant interpretations of the law. An interesting point is made in the Oxford Bible Commentary (OUP, 2001) that these verses, 25 & 26 (about David eating the shew bread), are possibly a later addition, as they do not fit the situation perfectly.

Next, in chapter 3 (vv. 1-5), without any explanation as to how this event followed from the previous one, we have Jesus entering a synagogue and healing a man's probably paralysed hand, although described as 'withered' by the writer. It should be noted that the text says that people were watching Jesus to see what he would do that day, which implies that Jesus was already an established figure whose activities warranted such surveillance. This, in turn, makes it clear that Mark is describing a later rather than a very early stage in the ministry of Jesus. His question (probably too clever to have been invented) about whether it was lawful to do good on the sabbath (v. 4), adds authenticity to the account. This question from Jesus makes it clear that a very important part of his ministry is reforming scribal interpretation, or, perhaps better, misinterpretation of the law. As may have often been the case, the disability of this man, who was said in an early tradition to have been a plasterer, might have been psychological in some degree, or akin, perhaps, to tennis elbow or repetitive strain injury, which would have been cured readily by the healing powers of Jesus. Once again, Jesus is showing us that the sabbath laws should not hinder people from doing good on that day. This fits well with the mission of Jesus and is, in effect, a direct challenge to the then religious authorities. This would account for their beginning to discuss how they might get rid of Jesus, although collaboration with the more or less gentile Herodians (v. 6) sounds less plausible. In all the brouhaha surrounding healing on the sabbath one should allow for the fact that the sabbath was by far the best day for meeting other people, in spite of legal restrictions on travel distances, as no one was at his place of work on that day – except shepherds?

The continuation, stating that great crowds were

following Jesus (v. 7), may well have been gathered from a fairly frequent occurrence reported by Peter, and not necessarily appropriately placed here. The seemingly wild claims that so many people were coming from all over the place suggest 'literary' fancy. However, Jesus's unprecedented powers to heal and exorcise will have become very widely known and definitely crowd-pulling. The claim that people said, or even shouted, that Jesus was the son of God (v. 11) seems likely to have been developed more by the imagination of the writer than to have been based on witnesses' information. There is a point of interest: Jesus told his fisherfolk disciples to have a boat ready for him (v. 9) to preach from, which implies that their ties with fishing were still sufficiently strong for this.[14] The need to preach unencumbered by the crowds, swollen by the sick who wanted to be healed by his touch or by contact with him, is a validating detail for the general situation described as surrounding Jesus.

There follows a retreat into the hills (v. 13), where Jesus is described as appointing twelve to do his work of healing and preaching. John's far more haphazard, and so far more realistic, account of the recruitment of disciples makes this particular version appear less convincing. The list[15] is more or less copied in Matthew and Luke. James and John, sons of Zebedee, are regularly labelled as hot-tempered or even ambitious and self-promoting, as Jesus called them Boanerges, sons of Thunder (v. 17). There is no evidence for their being hot-headed, apart from the attributed request to be either side of Jesus in his kingdom. It would seem far more likely that this nickname was conferred in jest, as has been pointed out already, and suggested the opposite.

We have now a description that would appear to be exaggerated: the pressing crowd in v. 20 was so dense that it was impossible even to eat – were there some people trying to have something to eat at that very moment? Did people eat 'on the hoof' then, as seems to be fairly common nowadays?

We have next the very curious non-sequitur in v. 21 that friends and relations thought that this meant Jesus had gone out of his mind: attracting dense crowds is not normally a sign of someone being mentally deranged. Thinking that Jesus had gone out of his mind is not what the Gospel writers will have wanted to say, so we may be absolutely certain that this is based on fact, but not one connected with this occasion: members of the family had thought that Jesus had lost his reason; his rampaging through the Temple and overthrowing money changers' tables would be a much more likely reason for that. This is a strong indication that Mark's chronology is wrong here.

However, we have a very important piece of evidence in v. 22: Jesus is accused of being able to cast out evil spirits because a devil has hold of him and he is in league with the prince of the devils. This verifies, effectively, Jesus's outstanding powers in this respect, as there would have been no reason, otherwise, for Jesus making the points, almost certainly correctly remembered by the witness, that a house divided against itself cannot stand (v. 25): an interchange very like this must have occurred; this is an example of how one may establish what is likely to be true in the Gospel and how to deduce that. In v. 27, the difficulty of reconciling the statement about one not being able to overcome a strong man until he has been tied up suggests even more authenticity as confusion in the mind of the writer is thereby signalled: one does not write down confusing sayings unless there is a source that cannot confidently be disregarded or contradicted. The representation of the strong man as Satan at the end of time is not clear enough for us to be sure that this is the connection being made. Twisting the interpretation so that the one who overcomes and ties up the strong man is seen as the exorcising power in Jesus, could be stretching the bounds of possibility, although we might hope that Jesus will exorcise Satan out of every one of us. Jesus will have said something akin to this, but what Jesus actually said will have been easier to interpret and will have been said in a way more obviously related to the situation.

We then learn in vv. 28-30 about further matters that do not really fit with the picture of an all-merciful, all-loving creator God: no sins would be unforgivable but some sins were worse than others, such as deliberately leading people away from God. Once again, important points are being made with incomplete understanding; the writer thinks them genuine but does not fully appreciate what their import might be. The confusion makes it clear that the writer is trying to record something that has a genuine base.

In verse 31, the account returns to the family thinking that they should take Jesus out of public life as his behaviour is bringing the family name into disrepute. There was the wonderful expansive response from Jesus, when he is told that members of his family are outside and want him – his telepathic powers have alerted him to exactly what their real intentions are – "You all are my mother, brothers and sisters" (v. 34). It is almost certainly significant that his father Joseph is not mentioned; Jesus had, in all probability, become the chief worker in the family building business on the death of his father some years before, hence one of the reasons for the family thinking Jesus was not quite right in the head: he had given up a well rewarded, well regarded job to go around preaching some new-fangled nonsense, which brought in no money at all. Jesus was saying effectively, in v. 35, that everyone of us who takes his teaching to heart is a member of his family.

Chapter 4 starts with Jesus once again preaching from a boat; a synagogue may have served well on a sabbath but other days required other solutions. One of the most readily remembered methods of teaching used by Jesus was the parable (metaphorical comparison). Its subject matter and structure held the attention of the listeners and made it difficult for them to forget while, at the same time, it provoked thought, just as Plato's dialogues were designed to arouse and hold attention while they provoked thought. It was also a way of presenting ideas to which Jews then were well accustomed, as explained by William Barclay (p. 81, ii); it made the abstract concrete. We now have Mark's presentation of the important parable in vv. 3-9 of the sower – there might have been a sower actually working for the audience to see then. This parable is felt by the Synoptic writers to be so valuable that we find it in Matthew 13:3-23 and in Luke 8:5-18; both these writers follow Mark in misinterpreting Jesus's intentions when he uses the parabolic form of teaching, as will be explained. In this parable we have an excellent summary of how different sorts of people reacted then to the teaching which Jesus 'sowed' and how many people deal with the 'evidence' now, when they are learning from the twists and turns in life. We start with the seed or word which falls onto the footpath (although the Greek says 'alongside' the path) where its growth is stopped almost at once because it is deemed a complete waste of time by the hearer or stamped on by others whose opinions, for whatever reason, are considered more valid than one's own: one should form and then hold opinions dispassionately, independently for oneself; this destruction of the life of the word is the action of Satan. The idea of birds eating the seed suits the seed falling beside the path better, but the interpretation remains the same, as this time the hearers of the word are quickly disabused by people known and respected by them, so that the word has no chance of taking root. Then we have the word falling on rocky ground where there is too little readiness on the part of the hearer fully to consider the evidence and mull over what it means, although the initial reaction is one of enthusiasm; later concerns, troubles, perceived peer-pressure and developments in life take precedence, so that what one has learned is shelved and becomes as good as forgotten. Then we have those for whom the thorns of self-devotion and advancement and reward are so exclusive of anything else that they have neither time nor inclination to assess the evidence adequately, if at all. Lastly, we have those with minds as open as those of children, who take the time and the trouble to consider all the evidence, without allowing the opinions of others or surrounding attractions to distract them from examining everything carefully; they then follow the teaching to be found in the word; as a result, like the recipients of the ten and five talents in that parable, they contribute to the lives and spiritual health of those around them according to their abilities (talents).

Unfortunately, the writer mistakes the reasons for the extensive use of parables and declares in vv. 11 & 12 that Jesus teaches in this form so that only an initiated and privileged few will actually understand; he has learnt of the passage in Isaiah 6:9-10, "Go and say to this people: 'Keep hearing, but do not understand; keep seeing, but do not perceive.' Dull this people's mind, stop their ears, and seal their eyes, lest they see with their eyes, and hear with their ears, and understand with their hearts, and turn and be healed,"[16] and does not realise that those who foretell the future may have got the basic elements right, but interpreted them incorrectly; the prediction here is of what is to be feared or even to be expected, but not of what is wanted by God. Jesus's message tells us God wants us to listen and try to understand; the parables provoke further thought and discussion, thus increasing both comprehension and memorability. This failure properly to appreciate the milieu in which Jesus taught, shows that the writer was possibly not a Jew, certainly not a Jew who had lived much in Palestine, and that he was using material which almost certainly had been provided by a Jew who had known the character of the area well; this view presented by the writer is quite contrary to the picture Jesus presents when he is considering the plight of the oppressed majority, whose condition so moves his compassion.

Jesus uses the parabolic form because it is memorable and not nearly so likely to be seriously distorted during transmission as more usual forms of narration are. A loving God does not deliberately mislead members of his creation. Any interpretation that suggests the contrary is plainly and desperately wrong: Jesus came to proclaim good news and this good news is clearly meant for as many people as possible, not just a small select minority. Indeed, Jesus is reported as saying, "Let him who has ears that work, hear (the word)." His message is, in effect, followed by the instruction: "Listen to the word unless you are mentally unable to do so." It is meant for absolutely anyone who is prepared to take the trouble to listen and understand: no special restrictions there.

Matthew and Luke follow Mark in suggesting that the parabolic form was used by Jesus so that only a specially selected few would understand the teaching. That they should follow such a mistaken line of thought makes it clear that they believed the source of Mark worthy of very high respect; they may well have thought that the authority of Peter underlay this Gospel.

Indeed, the continuation in v. 21 with Jesus saying that no one hides a lamp, so that it does not shed the light which it has been lit to provide, makes it clear that Jesus wants all people to hear and understand his message, so long as they can and are prepared to try. He is not hiding the lamp of his teaching with mumbo-jumbo under a bed of secrecy so that only an initiated few may benefit, which is what the writer of the Gospel seems to have been saying. However, the curious juxtaposing, with the explanation of the sower parable, of the idea of a lamp giving light for people to benefit from it and no secret remaining hidden, is clearly inappropriate; this demonstrates, almost indubitably, that the writer has received accounts of what Jesus has been remembered as saying, but the details have become disconnected, and possibly distorted, during transmission. He had these different strands and wanted to save them but, not knowing the facts, did not manage to produce a convincingly coherent arrangement. If the writer had been inventing, there would have been rather more logical cohesion in what he said.

This establishes that there was a tradition but that the writer had not understood everything properly. Just as a teacher can often learn more from a pupil's mistakes than from what the pupil gets right, so we may often learn, as was pointed out on p. 28 above, something useful from logical discontinuities in the Gospels. As argued there, we need the converse here: from the writers' indirections we are to find directions out. Jesus had indeed said something about what was being reported but there had been, probably, a chain of people in between the actual saying and the later recording of that saying. We need to realise this if we are to derive real benefit from the Gospels: when we recognise 'discontinuities' we can then try to work out what Jesus may have meant, even if we cannot work out what words he actually used. We are likely to discover that the Gospel writers' thinking was erroneous from time to time; this is when we can make useful deductions.

Jesus says in v. 22 that nothing will stay hidden but that the truth will inevitably be revealed in the end. Perhaps we should try to do only what we are happy for everyone to know about, as well as being pleased to remember it ourselves. There is also another corollary: God does not judge us as, everything being known, we find we are judging ourselves, which may indeed be a sort of hell. We may contrive to disregard, at least to some extent, the judgements made on us by others, but our own glaring self-judgement, when we cannot avoid making that judgement *and* feeling its totality, is another matter. We shall need God's help to forgive ourselves.

Jesus is then reported as saying in v. 24 that people should expect to be judged in return by the standards they employ when judging others. This is then followed by an elliptical non-sequitur in v. 25: 'For those who have will be given more, and those who have not will forfeit even what they have.' This seems to be making the point that those who have taken the trouble to understand the teaching of Jesus and then put it into practice will learn more and do better, while those who do not make sufficient effort to understand and practise may lose the little understanding they may have. This is not totally different from using muscles if one wants to keep them in useful condition. The fact that there is a non-sequitur, although the statements seem absolutely right, suggests that the writer is using genuinely sourced material without completely understanding the drift of it all. This is not unlike much of what happens now: we are bombarded with teaching from the Bible by people who have not managed properly to master exactly what the texts actually mean and how these texts have come to say what they say, often because the preachers are trying to confront complications that do not really exist. Jesus's teaching is simple, easy to understand; the difficulties, which do indeed exist, are in carrying out in practice what one should learn from the teaching, rather than in understanding what Jesus said and meant, in spite of the mistakes in many of the texts.

In vv. 26-29 we have unlikely comparisons between life as we know it, and what we are to deduce from that about God's kingdom. We have a man sowing seed and then a crop resulting without the sower knowing what is actually going on to produce the crop. Perhaps God is repeating the parable of the lilies (Matthew 6:28, and Luke 12:27) which produce beauty because they leave what they cannot master to God to deal with. We should do our very best and then consign the rest trustingly to God.

After that (v. 30) we have a picture of the kingdom starting from something very small – the mustard seed is by no means the smallest, even if reputed to be such – and becoming great enough for everyone from everywhere to benefit from its food and shade. With the mistaken compilation and claims that Jesus taught only in parables (vv. 33 & 34) we may be fairly sure that the writer is using genuinely sourced material, even if it was distorted during the passage from one person to another; if he had been making it up himself, he would have been likely to have demonstrated more clearly that he understood what he was at. Here, in the seed, is the beginning: the number hearing the teaching of Jesus is very small but his teaching will grow and spread, like the tree, so that all the nations of the earth may benefit eventually.

The chapter ends (vv. 35-41) with the crossing of the sea and the sudden squall. This seems to be a highly developed derivative of the event recounted in chapter 6, vv. 45-52, which in turn is probably the same event as that chronicled in John's Gospel 6:16-21; there is a sudden storm on this occasion when they are much closer to land than they had realised and when they thought the deformed figure of Jesus was his ghost. The reliability of Mark's version of the miracle is weakened by the claim that the boat was already filling up with water (v. 37): anyone who has experienced a boat filling up with water knows the devastating and inexorable rapidity with which the actual sinking often ensues. An important point to remember is that Jesus *appeared* to be walking on the sea, in the Gospel of John, when he was *actually* walking alongside it. This is yet another demonstration of the gap between what the first three Gospel writers say and the actual events they are telling us about. Nevertheless, it is likely that there were many crossings of the Sea of Galilee in boats and it is also very possible that there were sudden storms. One has to remember that when confidence is at a low ebb, threats seem far worse, while the coming of a calming confident voice may so lessen the atmosphere of menace that it as good as disappears altogether.

One may add to this that Jesus's sense of humour is very likely to have prompted him in v. 39 to instruct the wind and the waves to calm down, by way of a joke, but knowing the effect this would have on his followers. Unlike King Canute, who knew the sea would not obey his command to stop flowing in – only his silly (unless they were being very cunning) flattering courtiers might have thought it would – Jesus knew that his disciples would feel that the sea had indeed obeyed him.

Chapter 5 is introduced by the many-demon-possessed man in the country of the Gerasenes. The claims in this story that no chains could be found strong enough to hold him in v. 4 suggests exaggeration and some detachment from reality: the gap between event and recording is likely to have been considerable. Self-harming (v. 5) may well have been part of the problem as well as the description of there being a legion of demons. The details of Jesus being greeted with worship and the words attributed here (vv. 6 & 7) must be conjecture. The extra detail in v. 10 that the devils begged Jesus not to send him or them out of the country seems unrealistic and likely to have been dreamed up by the writer. More interesting is the idea of a herd of swine, vv. 10-13, becoming a new home for the devils. As it is improbable that devils wanted something to 'live in', something that would last for no more than a very few minutes, the actual line of the event is likely to have been different. Much more probable is the use by Jesus of his telepathic power. He will have persuaded the psychological case to believe he was seeing the swine stampeding and that his devils had left him in order to drive the herd of swine into the water. The 'patient' could 'see' he was no longer possessed by demons and so no longer had any excuse for demon-driven behaviour. Perhaps the herd of swine moved in a way that enabled Jesus to project an imagined vision of descent into water to effect the cure. Even though swine were not proper animals for Jews to keep, their destruction would not have been part of Jesus's programme of love, peace and life. Incidentally, a herd of about 2,000 pigs (v. 13) would require an enormous quantity of food, so this number might be hyperbolic.

It would seem likely that the healing of a seriously deranged man would cause very considerable amazement, but the description in vv. 14-17 of those astounded by the change in the man, the actions of the herdsmen and how they all reacted, may have been calculated by the writer rather than come from a witness, and, similarly, the request that Jesus should leave them and go elsewhere may have been the writer's elaboration also. However, the desire of the cured patient in v. 18 to become a follower of Jesus may well have been rightly recorded as we have Jesus saying in v. 19 that he would do the cause of reforming Judaism more good by spreading the good news in his home-territory than by becoming a follower of Jesus there and then. This would seem likely.

We often find the Gospel writers saying that Jesus told his patients not to tell anyone, which they mistakenly thought Jesus actually meant and expected; when Jesus told people not to tell anyone else he is very likely to have given this instruction with a cheerful smile, in the certain knowledge that exactly the opposite would happen. The idea, promoted by some commentators, that Jesus wanted fewer people coming to him is surely mistaken, as he had 'come' to help as many as possible so long as they were willing to be helped.

We next, when Jesus has crossed the sea, have the account, starting in v. 22, of the ruler of the synagogue begging Jesus to come and heal his daughter. At first reading one may be reminded of the courtier in John asking that his son be healed, but this time there are important differences suggesting that this is indeed a different occasion. Not only is the patient a girl but the ruler of the synagogue is named as Jairus. Literary invention was not, it would appear, one of the writer of Mark's strong points, so both being a ruler of a synagogue and named could be considered indications that there is a factual basis for this story. That the ruler of a synagogue, who held an important and highly regarded position in the community, should approach someone who was much lower in the class hierarchy, is very telling, particularly when it is coupled with the approach to Jesus by a courtier from the court of Herod Antipas, as related by John. Jesus's reputation was becoming powerful and pervasive, which will have been causing considerable concern to the religious authorities. An important strut in the argument for authenticity of both the 'miracles' is the interpolation in vv. 25-29 (see p. 51 above) of the woman with the haemorrhage being healed. There seems to be no need to add this real-life story to increase the effect, while the details are consistent with authenticity rather than literary 'faction'. A very important part of the story is the interchange in which Jesus points out that the girl is in a coma but is laughed out of court in v. 40. The writer probably thinks that the girl is indeed dead but we now know better. Jesus was telling everyone exactly what the true situation was: that the girl was in a coma. Commentators who want to think that Jesus was wrong to say she was still alive need to think again; it is they who are wrong, not Jesus. That the story is true supported by the circumstantial details that the girl was about twelve years old in v. 42, which was the cusp of womanhood – that started at twelve years and one day

– and that she should be given something to eat. Jesus's instructions in v. 43 that no one should be told about this can have been issued only in the full knowledge that the story would be spread with almost astonishing rapidity. Jesus will have been laughing quietly, if not actually out loud.

Chapter 6 now has us listening to Jesus in the synagogue or, rather, to those who wonder where his knowledge and understanding have come from (v. 2), seeing that he is merely an artisan (or craftsman) – or rather *was*, as he had given up the work. They all know Jesus (v. 3), just as they know all his brothers and sisters, who are present. Revealingly, not only is his mother, Mary, named, without Joseph being so, but also four brothers (James, Joses, Judas and Simon), while the sisters are neither named nor numbered. This highlights the importance of Jesus so often associating with women, who were considered by everyone else, as is shown by the writer here, as being without any real importance; at the same time, it is made clear, by implication, that Joseph is no longer alive. These doubters had forgotten that the prophets, in their past history, had similarly sprung up anywhere, inspired by God, and that Jesus's learning might, in like manner, have been coming straight from God. Jesus reminded them of prophets, when he declared in v. 4 that it was only in his own country (where he was considered to have been born) that a prophet was without honour.

It was, probably, of this particular passage that the writer of John was thinking when, in John 4:44, he inappropriately wrote that Jesus had declared that a prophet was without honour in his own country. However, the writer went on to correct this mistake on advice from his informant. The claim here in v. 6 that Jesus was amazed at their unbelief is clearly mistaken: it is everyone else, including the writer of the Gospel, who would have been amazed; Jesus understood his fellowmen far too well. Characteristically, Jesus's highest implied claim here is to being a prophet, nothing more, although, also, nothing less – he is sure his understanding comes straight from God.

The previous statement in v. 5 that Jesus could do no great work there is almost certainly the editorial fancy of the writer. Jesus's wonderful gifts were powerful anywhere, although, obviously, a lack of faith would weaken their effects to some extent.

We have in v. 7 the statement that Jesus sent his disciples out on missionary work with healing and exorcising powers. The probability of this happening in the manner related is undermined somewhat by the subsequent instructions in v. 11 to show disapprobation to any people in general, if only some of them failed to offer hospitality. Jesus would not have wanted the innocent to be condemned with the guilty; indeed Jesus, as far as we may gather, was not interested in condemnation at all, only in healing and goodwill. This instruction and sending out of The Twelve is repeated by Matthew 10:1-15, while Luke 10:1-12 expands the number to seventy; the sign in these subsequent accounts, which should make us wary, is the claim that Jesus declared that the fate of any people who failed to show due hospitality would be worse at judgement day than that of Sodom, to which name Matthew appears to have added Gomorrah. There is neither logic nor probability in these embellished endings, which reduces the overall credibility of the stories. The Marcan account of Jesus having sent out disciples to preach and heal receives some certification as to being authentic as they are said in v. 30 to have reported on what they said and did, while the omission of this missionary activity by the writer of John does not itself weaken the historical case for its having occurred. Indeed, the picture of disciples being as powerful as their master would not fit the picture the writer of John is trying to present; the witness behind John's Gospel might have been engaged elsewhere at the time, anyway.

With regard to the fate decreed for those who do not welcome those preaching in the name of Jesus, we might remember the ambivalence in John's Gospel about judgement, where Jesus is quoted as saying he does not judge but the writer says he does claim to do so after all. This suggests that the idea of a day of judgement has been introduced by the Gospel writers but not by what Jesus actually said at any time. Jesus's message was a positive one of goodwill linked with redemption (being lifted out of our evil ways into better lives) and salvation, not a negative one involving punishment and retribution. If Samuel Taylor Coleridge was right he presents an instructive picture very near the end of his 'Rime of the Ancient Mariner':

> Farewell, farewell! but this I tell
> To thee, thou Wedding-Guest!
> He prayeth well, who loveth well
> Both man and bird and beast.
>
> He prayeth best, who loveth best
> All things both great and small;
> For the dear God who loveth us,
> He made and loveth all.

The appearance, in vv. 14 & following, of the account of Herod Antipas's reaction to the activities of Jesus and his disciples, together with his treatment of John the Baptist, seems very plausible: it adds little to the picture the writer wants to present, so we may be fairly sure of its likely historical validity. However, Josephus's attribution to Herod of a fear of an improbable insurrection by the followers of John the Baptist, seems an unlikely reason for having John killed; Mark's account may make better sense. The scene in which Herod's step-daughter dances publicly, doing what was associated with prostitutes rather than respectable people, is sufficiently bizarre to be true: Mark was not a modern novelist. Herod did not like his amazingly immoral lifestyle being impugned publicly by John the Baptist, and Herodias, at once both wife and niece, if the dates fitted, would have disliked this even more. Being heavily critical *and* telling the truth is often unforgivable. The awkward point is that the accusation remains, even though it cannot be repeated by the one who is dead.

We now have the attempt (v. 31) to seek a rest from the crowds. John's account, which, although it does relate a withdrawal (6:1), does not go so far as to suggest that there was not enough time even for Jesus and his followers to eat, nor that they were very weary, so Mark's suggestion that this was the case could have been artistic licence. However, the Marcan version may still be right as the witness to John may not have appreciated the true situation since his own youthful energy was almost inexhaustible, while he was so taken up with the excitement of every moment that hunger would not have been noticed and he was far too young to see matters from the same point of view as his older companions.

At v. 34 we have the information that Jesus was moved by the crowd being like sheep without a shepherd. The teaching offered by the religious authorities was failing to provide them with any real spiritual nourishment and emotional support. We then have Jesus 'teaching many things' but we are given no idea what. It will have been, one presumes, the spiritual nourishment which they needed, including, no doubt, explanations of what the scribal interpretation of the law was hiding from their view.

As has been argued elsewhere, the tradition of the feeding of the five thousand, in vv. 35-44, although the actual number is likely to have been overestimated, is so firmly embedded that it is very difficult to dismiss. The extra detail given in the Johannine version indeed adds circumstantial evidence to strengthen claims to authenticity for the story. For instance, the question posed by Jesus to Philip in John 6:5-6 "From where do you think we might buy food for all the people?", (which is quite certain to have been airily asked as a joke) is omitted from the Marcan version, where the task of finding food for them all is set to the disciples, which sort of challenge does not fit the character of Jesus as presented in John. Mark also misses the proximity of Passover, which would explain both why there were so many people and why most of them would have had some provisions with them for emergencies. In addition, Mark, although he notes the grass was green where John notes it as plentiful, misses out the detail that the five loaves were of the cheapest variety (barley), suggesting, as is the case so often, that the most generous are the poor. John alone says that the boy was discovered by Andrew, Simon Peter's brother, another circumstantial detail. It is true that some argue that the skilful author of John invented these details to endow this account with verisimilitude. However, truth was frequently claimed to be hugely important to this author, so such invention should not be readily accepted as likely. John also left out the idea that it was the disciples rather than Jesus who distributed the food. The Johannine version has probability in its favour as the distribution was probably ceremonial in style, while it would be a boy, another detail missed by Mark, who will not have felt the inadequacy of his offering as being quite irrelevant and who will have offered his meagre supply in the first place. However, all the writers quote the sum of 200 denarii as being needed for so much food, a very considerable amount of money in those days. Curiously, English translations seem to think that the crowd was commanded to sit, when the Greek word, as well as the custom at the time, involved reclining in a semi-recumbent position, not sitting.

At v. 45 Mark seems to think that Jesus stayed behind to dismiss the crowd and had sent the disciples away in a boat, whereas John gives a much more unexpected reason, which makes much more sense: that Jesus could sense a swelling emotion in the crowd wanting to have him as their king. So, as one would expect, the crowd was left to dismiss itself.

V. 47 introduces the curious incident which ends with Jesus looking like a ghost walking on the water.

A late night squall has caught the boating disciples and has them struggling to progress and stay afloat. We recognise at once a failing on the part of the writer to understand Jesus when he imagines Jesus was walking as if he was going to pass by (v. 48) and leave them all helpless. Jesus had a sense of humour but not of that sort. The Johannine version is clearly the right one and this, a third hand version, has been redacted by the writer. The timing of the event demonstrates some difficulty: one might be able to walk round that part of the Sea of Galilee more quickly than a boat would be able to cross in adverse wind conditions, but that becomes far less likely if there is a good chunk of time devoted to prayer on the part of the walker while the boat is making the crossing. An illuminating ending to this incident is added by the writer of Matthew; he claims that the disciples now saw that Jesus was the 'Son of God.' Luke, who deals with the same event in 8:22-25, refrains from going as far as this, although there is great wonder that even the winds and waves obey him. It seems clear that the more mouths through which a story about Jesus comes, the more elaborate and far-fetched the details may become.

The last part of the chapter, beginning with v. 53, which tells how great multitudes of people wanted to have their sick relations, friends and acquaintances healed, makes very easy sense. This will have occurred almost anywhere, wherever Jesus went. However, this is the land of the Gerasenes, where Jesus had exorcised the legion of devils. The healed patient had evidently done a good job spreading the good news about Jesus. The extravagant claims about 'everyone' being healed might just be true but of that we cannot be sure.

Chapter 7 starts with what is almost certainly a true account of some communal dining event, in which the authorities complained about the failure of Jesus's disciples to adhere to the demanding detail of the 'legal' system involving religious cleanliness when eating, even if it did not occur at this point; it was these obsessional interpretations of the law from which Jesus had come to free them all. Washing one's hands when they are dirty is one thing, but having to go through a lengthy stipulated ritual every time before eating any particular thing was unnecessary. Barclay says that the detailed amplification of the law by the scribes began five hundred years or so before 'Christ', but Leviticus might, for some readers, have a date possibly even earlier than that, when one allows for the long period in which the book was developed before it reached its present form. Vv. 3-4 explain in some detail the legal requirements for eating according to scribal interpretation of the law. Barclay's excellent exposition of the hand-washing ritual in his commentary on Mark, pp. 165-9, sounds almost impossible to observe. Jesus taught sound sense where the scribes did not.

In vv. 6-7 Jesus points out that honouring God

properly is demonstrated in deeds, not adherence to ritual, however demanding the ritual may be, and next we have confirmation that something like what follows actually happened: the devastatingly apt quotation from Isaiah 29:13, which condemns those who honour God in ritual but not in actual deeds, would seem beyond the likelihood of any literary invention; it is much more likely to come from God than the mind of any mortal man. The superficial hypocritical behaviour bears comparison with the condemnation of the Church of Laodicea in the Book of Revelation 3:14-22 because they are merely going through the motions of being 'Christian' during their church attendance and not actually doing the good works outside the rituals, to which learning from those rituals is supposed to lead. However, the details that follow demonstrate the human limitations of the writer of that book, because the anthropomorphic ideas of regal reward in the 'next world' are clearly all too human in origin.

There follows, in that chapter 29 of Isaiah, the remarkable verse 16: "How perverse of you! Should the potter be regarded as the clay? Should the thing made say of its maker, 'He did not make me' and that formed say of him who formed it, 'He does not understand anything.'?" Atheists may need to examine all the available evidence dispassionately and very carefully, just in case they might be wrong. Greeks had worked out an atomic theory simply by observing the world around them and some of them had also calculated that there was something beyond this world which was somehow responsible for its existence. The Greeks appear to have been right about the constitution of matter and they might be right about why matter exists as well. We need to find convincing evidence before we reject this second proposition which entails the existence of God.

Tradition and hidebound thinking are not sufficient. We need to understand that we should do the thinking *before* we come to a decision and not *afterwards* when we use our intelligence to try to justify a possible mistake; this may be the position of some atheists. We should use our intelligence, studying all the evidence *dispassionately*, before we decide, rather than allow our emotions to hold sway, drive us into unfortunate decisions which then hold us chained by the consequences thereafter, while we waste our energy, intelligence and time trying to justify a foolish decision.

The continuation in vv. 9 & following provides even more powerful evidence that the teaching has come from Jesus and not the imagination of the writer. This is made clear by the detailed excoriation of the manner in which the flouting of the commandment, 'Honour your father and mother that your days may be long in the land!' was changed by a scribal 'tax avoidance' scheme: the money needed for helping parents is going to God instead, so there is no need to bother about them any longer. There is then the very interesting statement where Jesus points out in v. 20 that what comes out of the mouth defiles far more than what goes in. The implication is that their cleansing rituals should also be concerned even more with that.[17]

Once again, the profundity of the logical wisdom displayed in this devastating set of revolutionary statements shows quite clearly that this is a genuine example of Jesus's teaching and argument, and that the ultimate source for all this can be only God. The evidence for the divine source is not in mere claims but in actual outcome. Claims to divine authority need evidence, if they are to be considered credible. In this respect the teaching, arguments and deeds of Jesus are unique: their quality shows they come from God, not just from Jesus, a man.

In v. 14 there appears that all important explanation of what the rules about 'eating' should be: they are *not* about eating, about what goes into the mouth, but about what comes *out* of the mouth: the words with which we greet the world.

The scene is now changed in v. 24 to Tyre and Sidon, two well-separated independent cities on the coast, north of the Sea of Galilee and in Phoenicia, part of Syria. Even though this area was said to be an original part of the Promised Land, this is now Gentile territory, which suggests that Jesus is indeed interested in other people rather than only the Jews. We have an account in vv. 25-30 the details of which attest to authenticity.

However, the tone of the encounter with the Syrophoenician woman has not been well-understood by many commentators. Jesus would not have been at any stage in danger of causing offence, so when he said he had come to the Jews – he is in Gentile territory, so this is very clearly a joke – and not to look after the equivalent of pet dogs, he will have been mocking racially-minded Jews, not casting any aspersions on her. His understanding knew perfectly when humour would work, and he seems almost never to have resisted the onset of a joke; just as Harry Secombe and Dudley Moore never did. We may be sure that this meeting happened and that the outcome is very likely to have been positive: her sick daughter will have been cured of the unclean spirit, although how the evidence for this was passed back to Jesus and his disciples we are not told. The commentary on this passage in Barclay, pp. 179-83, is first class.

Jesus is now reported in v. 31 as going to the Decapolis, perhaps going north from Tyre to Sidon first before travelling south; it sounds as though the journey might have been getting on for a hundred miles, while nearly all the Decapolis area was Gentile, a nominal grouping of ten cities concerned with commercial co-operation. There someone was brought to Jesus for him to heal (v. 32). We cannot know the actual cause of the man's condition, described as deaf and having difficulty in speaking, but it is possible that an elective-mute might be thought deaf because an elective-mute may make noises without actually speaking. However, the use of spittle (v. 33) would suggest a deeper problem than just that. Barclay, in his commentary, pp.184-5, refers to Suetonius's 'Life of Vespasian' where, in chapter 7, Vespasian heals someone's blindness with his spittle applied to the patient's eyes, as in Mark 8:22-6 and John, chapter 9. A patient's belief in the efficacy of Jesus's spittle would probably have been extraordinarily powerful. The extra remarks about how everyone was amazed (v. 37) and their all declaring that Jesus had done everything well are very probably additions from the writer and not information about this individual occasion; these statements must be true but are likely to be general and so do not necessarily apply solely to this apparent miracle.

Chapter 8 begins with another mass feeding, this time four thousand (v. 9) and, in v. 5, seven loaves – the special number must give one pause – with a few small fishes mentioned later. Jesus's compassion for anyone in trouble was always in operation. The manner of presentation suggests that this might possibly be a garbled version of the feeding of the five thousand used by the writer to illustrate a favoured theme of his: how inadequate the disciples were. The writer does not understand that in denigrating the followers of Jesus, whom he has described as having been specially chosen, he is, in effect, denigrating Jesus (for an amplification of this see appendix 1). This is as clear a warning sign as one might require that the writer of the Gospel is very human and in error in this, his over-emphasised pet theory.

However, as has been shown, there are important points in this story. The Greek word for 'basket', in seven of which (v. 8) the leftovers were gathered up, is different from the word that was used for collecting the leftovers after the feeding of the five thousand (it was a specially Jewish basket there), which suggests that this is indeed a different occasion, although the number seven turns up to arouse suspicions. An arresting possibility, suggested by Barclay (pp. 187-8), is that if this was the same area in the Decapolis as that in which the 'legionary' demoniac had been cured, the size of the crowd might have been due to the missionary efforts of the cured man. After all, when he was reported as wanting to become a follower of Jesus, Jesus had told him, as we were reminded on p. 97, he would be more useful spreading the news there; perhaps this was yet more proof of the pudding.

The name of the next place in the itinerary is Dalmanutha (v. 10); its being apparently unidentifiable with any certainty now suggests the possibility of a genuine but 'misheard' tradition, which, in turn, might imply that the feeding of the four thousand is indeed a different occasion from that of the feeding of the five thousand. It is here, in v. 11, that the Pharisees are said to be asking for a sign. Barclay (p. 189) points out that this was an age in which signs or portents were eagerly sought (as Paul said in 1 Corinthians 1:22) to tell people that they should now expect great wonders heralding a messiah. The writer of John was using this desire when he decided that the basis of his Gospel should be seven signs and we also have a humorous allusion to this in John 4:48, when the courtier is begging Jesus to heal his son. Signs were near the top of the agenda then, just as money is clearly top of the agenda for many people nowadays. Jesus may have said something in v. 12 about not producing a sign, but the general claim that no sign would be given to this generation, when Jesus's very ministry was in itself a sign, makes it clear that the writer has got at least that detail wrong.

Thomas Edward Brown (1830-97) was a modern sign-writer:

A GARDEN is a lovesome thing, God wot!
Rose plot,
Fringed pool,
Ferned grot –
The veriest school
Of peace; and yet the fool
Contends that God is not –
Not God! in gardens! when the eve is cool?
Nay, but I have a sign:
'Tis very sure God walks in mine.

In v. 14 we have the occasion when, apparently, the disciples had tried and failed, or forgotten, to organise enough bread. There may well have been a number of times when there was not enough food for their needs. If Judas was both in charge of the money (John 12:6) and how it was spent he must have failed on these occasions, but would he have become sufficiently disgruntled to decide, eventually, to betray Jesus? One of these occasions might well have been used by Jesus to explain that the ways of thinking in the citadels of power, among the priestly authorities and in the political court of Herod, should be avoided, as these mindsets were like yeast, but giving rise to the wrong ideas (v. 15).

In v. 22 we have the healing of a blind man at Bethsaida. Again, as with the deaf and dumb man in chapter 7:32-5, we have the use of spittle in v. 23. There are similarities and important differences in this account of the healing of a blind man as compared with the account in John, chapter 9. Here we have a location, Bethsaida, but in John there is no location and the condition was described as 'from birth', while the parents of the patient were closely involved in the account. There are two witnesses for what may be the same event, while the differences are 'explained' by the sourcing of the material; the account in John was gathered from the vivid memories of a witness some six decades, perhaps, after the event, while that in Mark was probably a recorded account made during, or soon after hearing, Peter's teaching: Peter's memories are unlikely to have been nearly as accurate and detailed as those of the witness to John and the accounts will have come through more people. The reports are likely to be of the same event but they are clearly from quite different witnesses. The fact that there are two witnesses seems to validate the claims made: a blind man was healed with Jesus's spittle. Particularly arresting is the semi-cured patient's claim in v. 24 that he could see men as trees walking, before the final laying on of hands and Jesus's telepathic powers organising his neurological optical-control system completed the cure. This circumstantial detail will not, by any stretch of the imagination, have been dreamt up by the writer of the Gospel. It amounts to the final certification of the occurrence of the event.

The valedictory instructions in v. 26, to go straight home without going into the village, are more likely to have been an addition from the mindset of the writer, as there is no such instruction in the Johannnine version. Of course, this might, after all, have been a different occasion, when some 'medical' reason could have required the patient to go straight home.

In vv. 27 & following we now have another development, which sounds very plausible in general principle. Jesus was unique and people will have noticed this so Jesus might well have asked his disciples about what people were saying, although one should remember that the telepathic powers of Jesus were just about unprecedented and he will have known both what other people were thinking and what his disciples thought. Peter may have said, as the writer claims here, that Jesus was God's anointed one (a messiah), but we notice that even Mark does not attribute to Jesus any special claim to divine status on this occasion. However, we have his instruction in v. 30 that they should not allow their opinions to go any further, which sounds eminently sensible. Jesus is igniting quite enough trouble with the religious authorities without having any more combustible rumours being added to the fire.

We must beware, nonetheless, when we hear details of how Jesus is going to die, as in v. 31; we may be sure Jesus knew, by some means, that he would be killed, but not necessarily how, although we do have the amazing prediction in John 2:19 that his life would be restored on the third day. Nevertheless, even here we should be careful; Jesus may have given a less precise figure which this writer and others might have adjusted with hindsight. The claim that more or less certifies the general tenor of events as recounted in John is the crowd's statement that it had taken 46 years to build – actually rebuild or restore – the Temple; this sounds like fact, not fiction, as such plausible cunning was not in the character of the truth-seeking writer. An important pointer to the accuracy of John's story is the way in which the date of the interchange is fixed as 28AD, and so the date of the crucifixion as 30 AD, the date suggested by

Geza Vermes in an article in *The Guardian* in 2006, in which he makes clear his reasons for preferring John's account to those of the others. The restoration of the Temple had started in 19BC and, there being no year 0, 28AD was 46 years later and the Passover of the crucifixion a further two years away.

The grim foreboding and details may have come from the mind of the writer rather than from any evidence. The picture painted in John is less specific, although it starts to be made as early as chapter 8:21; here it is about Jesus returning to God, where he more naturally belongs, rather than on earth to which the rest of us naturally belong. This is illustrated by John earlier, in 8:14, when Jesus answers the Pharisees, ' "…because I know where I have come from, and where I am going … you, on the other hand, do not know where I have come from nor where I am going. "…[v. 21] (Jesus) said to them again, "I am going to go away and you will look for me, and you will die in your sin; where I am going you cannot come." ' Once again, these are much more likely to be the words of the writer than of the witness. However, it is in John, again, that we find the most reliable picture of Jesus anticipating his end, which is in the account of the Last Supper; here it seems that the ideas of betrayal and how it all might end are quite new to them. There was Peter's bewildered question of Jesus (chapter 13, v. 37), who has just declared that he was going where they could not go: "Lord, why cannot I follow you now? I will lay down my life for you." These words make it clear that Peter had no idea of what Jesus meant by 'going' nor of what was going to happen, even though he now realised that the 'going' had very ominous implications. If the disciples had been told as plainly as Mark outlines in vv. 31-2, they would have had a much better idea of what was going to happen than is presented in John. We may rely on John's account, which comes straight from the indelible and detailed memories of a witness. Mark's picture, which seems to have been based rather more on imaginative deduction than on factual evidence and witness, is likely to be misleading.

We have, all the same, an important indicator of the likelihood of something like this interchange in vv. 32-3 with his disciples having occurred: "Get thee behind me Satan! You are on the side of men, not God's." Simon Peter is the only one – apart from John who was probably, unknown to the writer of Mark, in Ephesus – who could have passed this on, while no one would have invented it. This reminds us that Jesus, even though he is under direction from God, is still only human and the terrible prospect of his death, perhaps rather less than a year away, would have been daunting indeed.

Vv. 34-8 end the chapter with Jesus telling his disciples and the others there that anyone who wants to excel, to be a true follower of his, should put the good of others before his own – which is indeed very probable – but not, surely, "Let him take up his *cross*!". Jesus is not telling us to deny ourselves, which is negative, but to be concerned for the good of others, which is positive. This has to be the writer's misleading fancy, fashioned after and by the eventual death of Jesus, while Jesus's saying that any who were ashamed to admit the truth of his teaching would find he (Jesus) was ashamed of them shows no understanding of the love, compassion for and understanding of his fellows on the part of Jesus. Jesus loves everyone, however bad we may be, however much we may fail. The anthropomorphic character of this passage demonstrates all too clearly its very human origins.

Chapter 9 starts with a very challenging claim that some of those hearing Jesus's words at that very moment would still be alive when the kingdom of God arrived with power. This might require a little care; we may be sure that the writer wrote what he believed to be true, but explaining how this might be so is not straightforward. Certainly this confirms the early and prevalent belief that Jesus would return so soon that no special written records of him and his teaching were needed. It was when he did not come back as soon as expected that written records began to be compiled. A curious explanation might be that just before the moment of death some of us may be lucky enough to 'meet' Jesus as we leave this life (see p. 38 above); the possibility that the writer understood and actually meant this would seem very remote.

The writer, we may therefore conclude, did not fully grasp the import of what he was stating and so we may infer that there is likely to be a genuine basis for the general idea that Jesus's teaching was to be spread with power. This might be said, then, to foreshadow the amazing missionary success of Saul (to be called Paul): the effects of the new religion were soon very widespread and, only thirty or so years later, prevalent enough in Rome to be noticed by many of the citizens. This is the more likely explanation, although it might not seem to fit the reported words of Jesus quite as well as could be wished.

We now have, in vv. 2-10, the amazing event described as the 'Transfiguration'. It is said to have taken place on a high mountain near Caesarea Philippi, where they were bound in 8:27; this must be Mount Hermon whose summit is over 9,200 feet. As on a number of occasions, Jesus took just Peter, whose brother, Andrew, may have been keeping the fishing business going, James and his brother John with him, possibly because they were the only ones readily available at the time.

The interesting point is that John, the witness behind the Fourth Gospel, is said to have been there but he did not, apparently, mention it to the writer of that Gospel. We may be confident that the writer would have chosen it as a sign if the witness had done so. We may also be fairly certain that Simon Peter told the source of Mark's Gospel what he had actually experienced, yet John seems not to have had the same experience; it would have been quite unforgettable.

The explanation may be fairly straightforward. The witness for John's Gospel was a very energetic youth but Simon Peter may have been a rather portly, somewhat older man. At over 9,000 feet, after a demanding ascent and in the noticeably thinner air, Simon Peter may well have experienced an hallucination, which, we assume, would have been prompted by God. We may be absolutely sure that it happened because, as has already been pointed out, the idea that they should construct three shelters *'for he did not know what to say'* (vv. 5-6) cannot otherwise be accounted for, as such invention is not in character and would be completely unprecedented for the literary style of the period. The Transfiguration indeed happened for Peter, but probably not for John. Further, we may calculate, as has been implied already, that God is likely to have induced Jesus to take the three up the high mountain specially so that Peter would experience this hallucination, even though John and, presumably, his elder brother, James, did not share it.

The detail in v. 7 that it ended with cloud enveloping Jesus, Moses and Elijah evokes the association of cloud with God, as detailed by Barclay (pp. 215-6) in his commentary; here he refers to examples of God appearing in a cloud to the Israelites in Exodus 16:10, 19:9, 33:9 as well as I Kings 8:10 where it fills the Holy

Place of of the House of the Lord. Cloud will have been associated in the Israelite mind with a messiah as well as with God. A cloudy end to his trance-like experience would seem both appropriate and plausible; the second half of v. 7, 'This is my beloved son, heed what he says!', however, wholly apposite though it be, is much more likely to have come from the imagination of either Peter or, more probably, that of the writer.

It is worth bearing in mind that Peter addressed Jesus as 'Rabbi' in v. 5. This is likely to be what Peter actually said, as the writer will probably have preserved the original information. This in no way conflicts with the thesis that Jesus's teaching comes from God, as we may be sure that the passage in John 6:68-9, where Peter says that Jesus has the words of eternal life, was quoted more or less verbatim to the writer and here it is clear that Peter knows that what Jesus teaches comes from God and that Jesus was the nearest thing to God on earth.

That Jesus should tell them in v. 9 not to tell anyone else about this seems absolutely right; the other two would have known that Peter had been affected differently from them but they will not have felt any need to ask for further explanation. It is true we understand that Mark may adjust what he has been told so as to present the message in what he feels is the most effective way, but how Jesus may have told them that they could report on this at a later date we cannot be sure of: we cannot discover with any certainty how detailed was Jesus's expectation of how he would actually die, nor of how he would appear to his followers afterwards. Nevertheless, it seems his knowledge of the future extended to his anticipating such explosive frustration on the part of the Romans with the Jews that it would end up with the Temple being more or less completely destroyed.

One should bear in mind that Jesus would have been all too aware of the bigoted intransigence of the orthodox and highly influential religious authorities, which more or less guaranteed a clash with the Roman rulers, and that, as the seat of the problem was in adamantine religious inflexibility, the Temple, the centre-piece of the Judaic religion, would almost certainly be destroyed, in the hopes that, thereby, the Jewish will to resist would also be crushed.

We have in v. 11 the question: 'Why do the scribes say that Elijah must come first?'. This may have been genuine or interjected by the writer to chime with the beginning of the Gospel where he introduced John the Baptist in the guise of Elijah. We have the curiously disconnected reply, when Jesus says in v. 12 that Elijah is indeed to come to *set everything right* and then adds, incongruously, 'How is it then, that the scriptures say of the Son of Man that he is to endure great suffering and be treated with contempt?' It seems that Jesus was referring to the 'Suffering Servant' in Isaiah (52:13-

53:12), which provides added confirmation that this chapter in Isaiah is indeed about him and not only about the people of Israel in general. The phrase 'Son of Man' (v. 7) is, quite obviously, Jesus's way of referring to himself, avoiding 'I' ('ego' in the Greek). Luke refers to this 'Suffering Servant' passage in Isaiah in Acts 8:26-34 which, in spite of Luke's genius for wonderful elaboration in his stories, is extremely likely to have had its original basis in fact. Indeed, the description of the person who was converted to Jesus's teaching as an Ethiopian eunuch by Luke enhances the likelihood of the truth being close to the actual account given, as such a person seems to add little to the lustre of the narrative of the occasion, while he seems to be an unlikely subject for literary invention. When Jesus says that 'Elijah has already come and they have done to him as they wanted', we cannot be sure that this is genuine or an interposition, as suggested at the start of the paragraph. It must refer to John the Baptist, anyway.

We next, in vv. 14-29, have the curing of the epileptic, which Jesus's other disciples had not been able to effect. We are introduced by an excited and devoted crowd running to greet their guru and the scene of a discussion between some of Jesus's disciples, none of whom is named, and scribal authorities. This event very usefully reminds us that for the people of Palestine at this time many diseases were said to be caused by demonic possession. Perhaps they thought this less easily attributable to some sort of sin on the part of the sufferer; as was noted in the first chapter, insanity is an excuse for every sort of sin. Epilepsy, being a neurological malfunction, might well have presented the sort of problem that Jesus's telepathic powers could sometimes cure fairly easily; this is, therefore, likely to be an account of an event that unfolded in a fashion similar to the description provided here. There is a part of this story that should be read with special understanding: in v. 19 Jesus is credited with saying, "What an unbelieving generation! How long shall I be with you? How long must I endure you? Bring him to me." If this is correctly recorded – as it may well be – Jesus will have had a cheerful, empathetic smile on his face; he will have said it all in jocular vein. "Bring him to me!" will have been said with a similarly joking sigh of resignation.

In verse 25 we have the strange idea that a crowd, which is already there, is *running* together. This would suggest some disconnection in the mind of the writer from the actual course of events, demonstrating clearly that the account is not based on firsthand evidence. Some of the details of the way the affliction worked may sound as if they have been moulded by a traditional viewpoint rather than stemming directly from a witness, so, for instance, it might be that the idea that it was the demon who shrieked through the mouth of the afflicted in v. 26 was what the writer believed must have happened and, possibly, even what any witnesses to the occurrence thought, in spite of the fact that it would seem unlikely that the course of the fit really happened in this way. There is, however, one circumstantial detail that seems to validate the general line of the story (v. 24): "I do have faith; help me where my faith falls short!" uttered by a desperate father. This would, otherwise, be an example of imaginative invention well beyond what one should expect of the writer. We end in v. 27 with Jesus helping the seemingly dead patient up after his latest epileptic fit, his healing hands completing the cure.

When the disciples, who had failed to exorcise the demon, asked in v. 28 why they had failed, and Jesus responded with the explanation that much practice in prayer was needed first, this is understood when one remembers that 'healing hands' may be possessed by someone but that it would seem likely that if that person were able to improve his (or her) ability to 'listen' to God, that would make him (or her) work better; one achieves this by praying to God more effectively, more assiduously, as Jesus is said to have advised his disciples here in v. 29.

We now have in v. 31 somewhat more precise prophecies attributed to Jesus, about his death and resurrection. The failure of the disciples to understand such a brilliant teacher suggests that what Jesus actually said was less definite and so less clear in the mind of Jesus than in the mind and writing of the writer of the Gospel.

The most reliable witness, it is argued, is the source of John. The picture presented in that Gospel is somewhat different and very mixed. Nonetheless, there is a clear reference to death and resurrection after the cleansing of the Temple, very early in the ministry, which is validated by the curious ambiguity of what Jesus meant and appeared to his hearers to have meant. He talked of destroying the Temple, when he meant the temple of his own body, and that his body would be restored – by him? – in three days; this number might have been put in by the writer but there is the curious confirmation of this number in the interchange in Mark's account of the trial in 14:58. This suggests that the account in John 2:19 is based on what Jesus must have said originally. Indeed, the exclamation by Jesus's hearers that it had taken forty-six years (John 2:20) to restore the Temple more or less guarantees that this interchange occurred. In John, otherwise, we have fairly frequent references to the 'Jews' wanting to kill Jesus, without mentioning a resurrection in three days. However, after that there are frequent claims on the part of Jesus that people wanted to kill him; there are accounts of intended stonings, of arrests being ordered, of Jesus going where they would not be able to go or find him. On the other hand, when we read of sayings such as "When you have lifted up the Son of Man", we may suspect that the writer of John is inserting his ideas rather than what he has actually learned from the witness. He was very keen to emphasise the idea of Jesus being lifted up. First it referred to the lifting up or erecting of the emblem of a serpent, which Moses had been instructed to make by God in Numbers 21:8. This was to save the Israelites who looked on it from suffering and dying after being bitten by the serpents; secondly, it promoted the idea that, for Jesus, the crucifixion, otherwise the most demeaning manner of execution, was, on the contrary, a form of exaltation. Jesus was being exalted and was saving the world that looked on him, and learnt from him, at the same time. The main prediction of his approaching death is made at the Last Supper, when Jesus knew that Judas was going to lead the High Priest's officers to where he would be. Then his telepathic powers would probably have alerted him as to how he was to die.

In Mark, therefore, there is an informative theme which combines Jesus foretelling his death and the disciples not understanding what he had said. The future was unclear and not known in detail, so we see that Mark's assessment was mistaken. Jesus was an outstanding teacher, as has been said already; what Jesus said must have been undefined in his mind and so unclear in expression; this 'aporia' adds authentication. Another point that validates the probable authenticity is the two-pronged addition: the disciples were afraid (v. 32) to ask exactly what Jesus meant and Jesus will have known that they were non-plussed. This means that Jesus did not want them to know the truth at that very moment and that he was not completely certain of the detail of it himself anyway.

We have now, in vv. 33-5, an entirely predictable episode: who was to be the greatest? Jesus will have known exactly what they had been talking about when he asked them about it. It was to answer precisely such a question that Jesus washed the feet of his disciples in the Johannine account of the Last Supper. Mark introduces a child in v. 36, who seems most conveniently to have been on hand; but how receiving a child in the name of Jesus answers this question is rather less clear, which suggests that the 'child part' of the incident might have occurred on a different occasion.

The next event, in vv. 38-40, seems also to be entirely predictable. Someone, enthused by the teaching and example of Jesus, was exorcising in his name; however, as he was not thought to be a follower or a disciple of Jesus, he could have been operating without proper authority. The fact that it was John who put the original question demonstrates perfectly his character: he was a devoted and hugely enthusiastic follower, who was always keen, like any curious child, to know what Jesus judged to be right in any situation, the opposite to being an aggressive self-promoter. Here the answer is not that those who are not for one are against one – which is not wholly logical – but the other way round: Jesus said, "He who is not against us is (as good as) on our side." This is very likely to have happened.

We have the somewhat disconnected addition in v. 41 that anyone who gives someone a drink in Jesus's name, or, rather, following the teaching of Jesus, will be rewarded. This does not seem really to belong here but it fits well with the teaching of Jesus in general. However, succeeding from the parable of the 'Sheep and the Goats' (pp. 15-16), it is probably following the precepts of Jesus which matters here rather than doing good in Jesus's name. It is doing good that is important, while Jesus's teaching tells us how to feel and behave so that we actually do what is good.

After this, in v. 42, we have the condemnation of anyone who leads a child away from faith in the God whom Jesus is telling us about. Once again, we may suspect that the account has been moulded to some extent by the mind of the writer: Jesus was positive rather than negative; doing good was far more important than being punished for failing, or actually doing evil. The interlude in vv. 43-47 about self-dismemberment is quite obviously about escaping from ingrained habits when they are the cause of error: however much part of one's life a habit or addiction may be, if it gets in the way of doing positive good, one must do one's best to rid oneself of it.

We have next a piece about salt (vv. 49-50). As it appears in the text it is not easily explicable. One has to deduce that there was probably a trustworthy source for the theme but that the correct way of presenting it was lost during transmission. Luke has this theme in 14:34. Barclay, probably correctly, points out that sayings of Jesus were often remembered by their themes and not context; so sometimes they were presented without a proper defining context by the writers of the Gospels. Sacrificial victims, salt and refining fire belonged together. We may draw different ideas from theses two verses. Religious teaching and belief, if they lose meaning, because they are being practised without purpose, without real sincerity, are no more useful than counterfeit, flavourless salt. Salt was important in those days and in that region. It was required on any sacrificial victim due to be burnt, so connecting it with Jesus's teaching would seem appropriate; it was a very important preservative, so prolonging useful life goes well with the teaching of Jesus too; it brought out the flavour of foods, as the teaching of Jesus might flavour our deeds.

Chapter 10 takes us south from Galilee into Judaea, from unsophisticated peasantry to cosmopolitan sophistication in the area around Jerusalem. When questioned by religious authorities in v. 2 about divorce, Jesus displays such astute command of the question that any doubt that inspiration from God was the source of his learning seems very difficult to justify. He knows that his teaching is considered heretical by many of them and that such heresy is a capital offence, so he refers them, in v. 3, first to Moses; nothing heretical there.

The actual passage, from Deuteronomy 24:1, states: 'If a man has taken a woman in marriage, but she does not win his favour because he finds something offensive in her and he writes a certificate of divorce, gives it her and dismisses her...'. The woman has neither say nor any rights in this. V. 12, in which Mark suggests that a woman may divorce her husband, is clearly from a non-Jewish mind: the source of the Gospel's information is *not* a knowledgeable Jew (Wilson, p. 36). It is true that some interpretations of this allowed only unchastity to be the cause of offence, but most interpretations were far more lax and completely in favour of the man; the lady had no more rights than a piece of property. One might remember that even in 1918, when women were at last allowed the right to vote in the UK, although the man could vote when 21 years old, the woman had to be 30. Proper respect for women is recent and still far from universal, as the dubiously motivated Taliban males in Afghanistan so callously demonstrate. The attitude to women seems little different in Iran where the supposedly God-directed religious rulers so flagrantly disregard human rights, or, rather, their responsibilities to other people, especially to women.

Here, Jesus, in effect, manages both to contradict the law of Moses and avoid possible charges of heresy by explaining that it was because of their own weakness when influenced by other attractions, their selfishness or hardness of heart (v. 5), that Moses had allowed for a certificate of divorce so that a man might get rid of his wife. However, using the earliest part of the Torah in Genesis (1:27 & 2:23-4), Jesus showed in vv. 6-9, that marriage was so powerful an act of unification in God's name that only God might be considered able legally to break it: 'What God hath joined together let no (mere) man put asunder.'

They may hate the teaching of Jesus, they may be urgent to find fault in it, but they cannot. Their years of devoted learning and application to mastering, to interpreting scripture, collapse under the overwhelming command of Jesus, who is an untutored Galilean artisan. Only God may know the reason for that. So surprising is this turn that brilliantly inspired literary fiction cannot be considered a satisfactory explanation; the story must be based in fact.

William Barclay, in his commentary on Mark, pp. 245-9, suggests that the definitive version of Jesus's ruling, on this occasion, is to be found in Matthew 19:3-9. On this Barclay provides a very full survey on pp. 228-45 in vol. 2 of his book on the Gospel of Matthew. Perhaps Malachi 2:16, as referred to by Barclay, should have the last word: 'If a man divorces his wife, says the Lord God of Israel, he overwhelms her with cruelty, says the Lord of Hosts. Keep watch on your spirit, and do not be unfaithful.'

Vv. 13-16 introduce a powerful point: children have a special attraction for many and to turn them away from Jesus, who loved women and children, seems quite wrong. Jesus was a teacher and the open-mindedness of children to learning new ways of thinking makes them wonderfully appealing. As Jesus says in v. 35, it would be good for us all to have minds as open as those of children when vital truth is there to be found and explored: that is how to come to understand the teaching of Jesus and carry it out.

There comes in vv. 17-22 the story of the rich young man, referred to on p. 48 above, where multiple strands of thinking lie behind the episode. At first glance, the interpretation is easy. A life devoted to enriching only oneself, rather than enriching the lives of those around one, is all too obviously being misspent. All possessions, mental and material, are responsibilities, which we should use to create and spread as much good in the world as possible; we are not supposed, like the man entrusted with one talent, to keep responsibilities, disguised as possessions, unfulfilled uselessly to ourselves. However, there is another strand which might be missed: some rich people have a retinue of servants whose way of life is dependent on the employment and care bestowed by a rich employer. These rich people are, like some of the Dukes of Westminster or the last Philip Yorke of Errdig, wonderful contributors to the livelihood of many. When this Philip Yorke discovered that the last surviving Yorke, then in Australia, to whom he had intended to bequeath his estate, had died, he was persuaded by a cousin who was staying with him, to give it all to the National Trust, which he then did. His concern and esteem for all the servants is splendidly recorded by the photographs which he had taken and which may be seen in the house. He was the head of a family of equals rather than a lord and master.

Jesus makes it clear in v. 25 that our responsibilities may so occupy our minds that we fail to live as we should: it is easier for a camel – the original word must have meant rope – to pass through the eye of a needle than for a rich man to enter the kingdom of God. The mistaken use of 'camel' instead of 'rope' demonstrates that this is based on an actual saying of Jesus; the incident has been passed on without proper understanding. We should realise at once that the 'Kingdom of God' is about us all fulfilling God's will, as when we pray, 'Thy will be done.' We then have something in v. 27 which might have come from the mind of the writer but which might also have come from an actual saying of Jesus: 'For all things are possible with God.' This has to be true anyway. The authenticity of this story is supported by the quite unnecessary detail that Jesus loved the rich young man.

V. 28 presents a serious challenge where Peter is credited with saying that they, the disciples, had given up everything to follow Jesus, apparently implying the complete abandonment of all previous links to fishing. There are two guides that caution against the idea that

Peter had given up fishing altogether, although it is clear that, in this last year of the ministry, he had spent much less time doing it. St Paul, a skilled worker with leather, as a tent-maker, who knew Peter well, makes it clear in his second letter to the Thessalonians 3:7-9, and elsewhere, that he expected preachers to earn their keep, suggesting that Peter had continued to earn something, while ties with fishing seemed always to be in the background. We note this especially when Peter, at the end of John's Gospel, proposed a fishing trip. He would not have done this if he and the rest of the fishermen had given up fishing completely. Why would he still have had a boat if he had given up fishing? The disciples had indeed given up a very great deal, but probably not their trade altogether. The writer will have written what he believed to be true, but he did not know all the facts. We, however, can most profitably deduce enough to correct the record and work out what is likely to be the truth.

V. 32 returns to the journey to Jerusalem and death – the disciples were in a state of fear. We may be sure that Peter was a likely source for some of the information, but the presentation and detail is probably due to the writer. We then have in v. 35 the interposition of a request from the brothers, James and John, that they may sit on either side of Jesus in his kingdom. It would seem possible that this was a 'literary' addition to go with their nickname 'Boanerges'. However, such a request is more likely to come from those who lack confidence than those who are brimful with it. Nothing we learn of the duo later seems to support the idea that they were aggressively self-promoting. However, the related interchange seems to contain truth; Jesus's reply to their request (v. 38) lacks the character of literary artifice, so there is likely to have been some sort of interchange like this. We then have the problem of working out what Jesus was actually referring to when he spoke of the cup from which he would drink, the baptism with which he had been baptised and the kingdom that would be assigned to him. Would spiritual inebriation from successful preaching of Jesus's message be the cup from which they would drink? Interestingly, James was indeed executed by Herod Agrippa in 44 AD, presumably for preaching successfully.

The sequel that there was indignation (v. 41) against James and John suggests that there is a solid foundation for this episode having occurred in some form. However, it is those who are less sure of themselves who are more likely to ask for 'promotion' rather than those who are more self-confident. Matthew has the same story, but this time it is the mother who is the petitioner; the fact that she is unnamed suggests that this is Matthew's way of making the two brothers appear less culpable while he was taking the story from Mark.

Jesus, characteristically, in vv. 43-5, uses the occasion to explain that it is not glory which matters but what one does to merit that glory. Profitable service to others, executed with goodwill, is crowning glory, and it is the service which matters, not the glory.

Next (v. 46) we have Jesus coming to Jericho, possibly not only the oldest town in the world but also the lowest at nearly a thousand feet below sea level. Jerusalem, whither he was destined, may be about three hundred feet lower than Safed in Northern Israel, but it is still, at nearly two thousand five hundred feet, a very high city. For comparison, the highest town in England, at about a thousand feet, is Buxton in Derbyshire. Jesus was going from the depths to the heights. Here, in Jericho (vv. 46-52), as if prophetically, Jesus gives sight to the partially blind son of Timaeus, for his crucifixion may be said to herald his giving spiritual sight to the world. The claim that Timaeus addressed Jesus as son of David sounds as though it is from the mind of the writer rather than that of a witness, while it would appear that the blindness was partial as he could see enough to reach Jesus without bumping into anything. However, it is true that Ved Mehta, who had been blind from the age of four, could sense where he was when he was a resident student in Balliol in 1957, and he would have had no such problem. Another point of interest is that in other cases of blindness being cured Jesus used his spittle, but here the problem seems to have been almost solely psychological. Jesus's over-ruling those who wanted to stop Bartimaeus from importuning him is characteristic, and so adds a certificate of authenticity to the story.

Chapter 11 starts with a challenge: Jericho is about 15 difficult, dreary miles from Bethany and the author of this Gospel seems to write as if they are a little closer together than that, for, immediately after being in Jericho, the party is described as approaching Jerusalem. Mark's order of events may be wrong here. The right order is to be found in John's Gospel. In that, after the raising of Lazarus, Jesus withdrew to Ephraim, about 14 miles north of Jerusalem because of the decision by the Sanhedrin to have Jesus eliminated. Six days before Passover we have Jesus back in Jerusalem, the crowds wanting to see Lazarus, raised from the dead, and 'Palm Sunday'. This all makes good chronological sense.

In vv. 1-6 we have the curious incident of the ass, riding which, while entering Jerusalem, fits so well with Old Testament prophecy (Zechariah, 9:9) as noted in Matthew, but, although there is indeed the possibility that Jesus had foreseen what was to happen and might even have arranged it, the simpler account in John, where Jesus happens to be near an ass and decides – Jesus and owner of the ass directed by God? – to sit on it, sounds more likely: the 'extras' in the Synoptics have the appearance of being 'decorations', particularly as Matthew's account is more elaborate than Mark's, and Luke's, quite predictably, is more elaborate still. The crowds massing around Jesus might have induced the owner of the ass to offer it to help, and he may have accompanied Jesus until he reached his destination, which might have been the Zebedee Jerusalem house, so as to ensure a safe return for his animal. The crowd's crying out 'Hosannah' (v. 9) – 'save (us) now' – harks back to the crowd's reaction after the feeding of the five thousand, as recorded in John, when they realised that the special powers of Jesus were exactly what they wanted in their leaders and believed that it was Jesus who could save them from religious and economic oppression. The extra parts of the accolade in v. 10, suggesting that Jesus was to save Israel as messiah (cf I Samuel 10:1 and 16:13 for Saul and David respectively) may well have been added decorations. A point of interest is that where John has palm tree branches (12:13) Mark has, much less specifically, 'leafy branches' (twigs cut from fields) and John makes no mention of garments being spread in Jesus's path.

Judas, nicknamed Maccabeus[18], after freeing Israel from the aggressively enforced pagan practices of the Seleucid Antiochus IV Epiphanes of Syria, had been similarly welcomed about a hundred and ninety years earlier. Hanukkah (Chanukah), the Feast of Lights, which coincided with the lead up to Christmas in 2022, still celebrates the restoration of the Temple today, even though, contrary to every reasonable desire and logical expectation, the site is still crowned with an alien building that does not appropriately celebrate the

God of the Hebrews, as Israel must regret; there should be the Temple to the God of the Hebrews there, not a mosque, as seems to have been foreseen in 13:14. The first Muslim house of prayer, preceding the mosque, was erected there under the auspices of Muslims in the 7th century following the death of the prophet Muhammad in Jerusalem; Israel is a free state now and so should be free to undo the injuries inflicted in the past; perhaps, with mutual agreement, the mosque should be moved to a more appropriate site.

In v. 11 we have Jesus entering the temple late in the day before going to Bethany (v. 11). There is no need to make this claim; it adds nothing to the picture the writer wants to paint; so this is very likely to have happened. But the suggestion that Jesus might have been surveying the area in preparation for his cleansing the Temple the next day would seem less likely, unless this was to be for the second time. John would probably have said this had it been so. The little story of the fig tree in vv. 13-4 and then vv. 20-1 sounds very much in character as to the beginning, but not as to the out-turn the next day. Jesus was quite possibly joking when he said he was hungry; he will have known that any figs on it would be tiny, inedible, while awaiting growth and ripening later. He probably said what he is credited with saying, but only as a jest, but the subsequent withering to death of the fig tree is quite out of tune with the spirit of Jesus; that would seem far less likely. However, there is a problem for this line of thinking as it is Peter who, on the next day, is said to have seen that the fig tree had died. Perhaps, for some reason, the fig tree did really wither, and Jesus might have been able to tell that it was just about to die. Jesus never intentionally killed any living thing nor taught people to kill anything. He never indulged himself in whims at the expense of others. Matthew's claim (21:19) that the fig tree withered and died at once is clearly quite implausible invention.

In v. 15 the Marcan version of the cleansing of the Temple starts, and it lacks some of the detail in the Johannine account, although we have a curious addition in v. 16 that Jesus would not allow anything to be carried through the Temple precincts – this was the court of the Gentiles, the furthest they were allowed to go; this was where a Gentile might pray. How did Jesus do this? The lack of further explanation suggests that this is a decoration added by the writer. However, there *was* a short cut through the Temple precincts which people were not supposed to use except for Temple attendance. Perhaps it was with reference to this that Mark said Jesus would not allow people to take their goods through. The instruction that they should not be making the Temple a den of thieves as it should be called a house of prayer (Isaiah, 56:7) is very possibly divinely inspired: how could Gentiles pray properly amid the noise of market traders?

The claim (v. 18) that the religious authorities feared the power and effects of Jesus's teaching makes sense, but it is the raising of Lazarus that would have brought this about, rather than an occasion when Jesus had apparently lost his reason, as his manner of cleansing the Temple would seem to have indicated; being mad is not a threat, but being a mighty miracle-making prophet and teacher is.

After the loss of the fig tree (vv. 20-1), which is prophetically placed by Mark after the cleansing of the Temple – the way in which Judaism was practised then was bearing no fruit – we have, in vv. 22 & following, the claim from Jesus that faith in God can help us overcome every difficulty (removing mountains in rabbinic teaching) which may be claimed by some to be true: when people feel that God is with them they feel that prayer not only deprives difficulties of all their menace but also shows them possible solutions. The extension, that whatever they ask for in prayer to God will be granted is clearly wrong, as one must be praying for what is best for building God's kingdom here on earth and no human can know exactly what that might be; the nearest we can manage is, "Thy kingdom come; thy will be done in earth as it is in heaven." Here, 'in' is to be preferred to 'on' as 'in' involves every molecule of the world's existence whereas the meaning of 'on' is much less inclusive. We may, and indeed almost certainly should, pray, and when we pray that God be with us, helping us to see how to make the world a better place, we may expect help, but when we pray for something else we may not be so sure that the prayer will be answered in the way we hope and desire, as our knowledge of the scene is but partial. An important point is made by Jesus about our forgiving others for what we perceive as wrongs against us: not only do grudges harm those who continue to bear them, but if we have had no practice in forgiving others we might have difficulty in forgiving ourselves when we come to see our own failures with ineluctable, inexorable clarity and detail. God, on the other hand, has already forgiven us even before we have done any wrong.

We now have the possibly misleading parabolic idea in vv. 23-24 of being able to have mountains cast into the sea. The writer seems not fully to realise that mountains represented difficulties and it was the riddance or diminution of difficulties that required faith in one's guide, God. Mark's version seems to suggest devastating the landscape, which cannot be right. We have, in v. 25, the added non-sequitur that one should forgive people for anything that they may have done to offend one. The idea that God is the one who forgives would seem to be misleading. V. 26, 'But if you do not forgive neither will your Father which is in heaven forgive your trespasses', is, therefore, probably a misleading addition; loving fathers have forgiven the sinner before the sins are committed. It is help to forgive ourselves that we need, and we get that from our practice in forgiving others.

Vv. 27-33: Jesus is again in Jerusalem and is being questioned by representatives of the religious authorities. Yet again, there can be no certainty that the chronology is right, although the tenor of the interchange is almost certainly based on something that did indeed occur. However, most commentators have missed the sense of humour which almost certainly underlay it all. The authorities were very serious and Jesus will have been making fun of their attitude with his teasing question about where the authority of John the Baptist had come from. The first unspoken part of the reply is, "Did you ask John about where his authority is derived from, as you are now asking me?" Almost certainly they had not asked him, so they, perhaps, should not now be asking Jesus this question. One can imagine the smile on Jesus's face as he asks about what they thought the source of John's authority might be. One suspects that the real reason for their not answering this question was fear of making themselves appear foolish before Jesus, as they would have been far more afraid of that than of the opinions of the inconsequential people who were slaves, or at least supposed to be, to their religious tyranny. Jesus will have had laughter written all over his face when he said that, as they would not answer his question, there was no reason why he should answer theirs.

Chapter 12 starts with a parable, almost certainly derived from the memory of Peter or some other hearer, in which the vineyard, representing the world, has been 'built' and furnished with every aid and then handed over to the Jews and the rest of us to care for. God sent representatives (prophets) to advise the rulers and peoples how to manage the world, so that it would produce the fruits which God's kingdom here on earth is intended to produce. These representatives were ignored, ill-treated or even killed, so God sent his only Son (v. 6) to help sort out the mess and, as we know, they killed him too. However, God arranged for this only direct representative of his ever to exist on earth to reappear for a considerable number of days after his death, to chosen people, who had believed in his divine mission, and to one, his brother James, who had not believed until Jesus had reappeared to him too, as recounted by Paul. An interesting suggestion might be to liken those who kill the only son in the parable to those who try to kill belief in God. Atheists argue, in effect, that the vineyard, or, rather, the world, as they have abolished any idea of God, belongs to us in a way that entitles everyone, or rather them, the atheists, to do whatever they like with it. Belief in God means the human race is responsible to God for what it does with the world. The ultimate owner of the world is God and not we; we are responsible to God for keeping everything in good condition and working well. We need to be open to inspiration from God for us to know how to do this as well as possible. Of course, a loving God will not vengefully come and destroy, but the action of the desecrators of the vineyard is a form of suicide, as climate change is now demonstrating all too palpably.

V.10 introduces the idea of the rejected stone becoming the most important one, while Jesus implies *he* is the rejected stone, which will later become the cornerstone of the structure of truth in religious belief. This quotation from Psalm 118:22, as the precise relation to the previous theme is not made clear, may have been garnered from a different occasion, or, of course, the vital connecting arguments may have been lost in transmission. Here, as Cole points out, we have the ironical question, put by Jesus to the scribes, self-professed experts in religious texts: 'Have you not read the scripture?' The additional comment in v. 12 that they wanted to have Jesus arrested would apply to any of the occasions when Jesus proved stronger in argument for the truth than they. This is likely to have come from the mind of the writer rather than from the information provided about this particular occasion.

In vv. 13-17 comes the celebrated question asked of Jesus by the religious authorities, "Is it right to pay tribute to Caesar or not?" The background to this question was the principle that the Jews were the subjects of God, first and foremost, and so could not rightfully serve any other ruler, while paying tribute to any other ruler implied subservience to that ruler, such subservience being against the Jewish law. The questioners had Jesus trapped: whatever answer he produced he would either be siding with Caesar, against the Judaic law, or be against Caesar, by saying tribute should not be paid. Jesus could not by any means avoid being condemned.

Jesus is unlikely to have had any money, any coin available, so he asks someone to provide a coin. When the head of Caesar is seen on it, making Caesar the residual owner, the possessor himself is at once guilty, merely through possessing the coin, of tacitly admitting subservience to a ruler other than God. In the Temple, of course, only Jewish money was legally accepted, although coins with the head of Caesar on them could be exchanged in the Court of the Gentiles for the 'right' ones, at exorbitant rates. Outside the Temple the religious authorities did not have jurisdiction although, on religious principle, they were supposed to claim they did. All Jesus had to ask then was, in effect, who the issuer of the coin was, and so owner in the last resort.

Possessing the coin and admitting to this, and that thereby the coin might be used, was tantamount to an admission of transgression of the Jewish law: the coin belonged to the jurisdiction of Caesar; the owner accepted this fact by just having the coin. Jesus's reply, "Give Caesar what is his and give God what is God's", cannot then be countered. So brilliantly unexpected is this line of thinking that literary invention may be ruled out with complete confidence: it was witnessed and passed along a chain of one or more people, to the writer. One might remember here that the man who produced this example of staggeringly quick-witted genius had been only an artisan joiner-builder; inspiration from God would explain it all.

Next, vv. 18-27, we are told about the Sadducees asking another celebrated question. We are reminded that the Sadducees – the very wealthy group that ran the Temple and collaborated with the Romans – did not believe in the resurrection of the dead, although the majority of Jews did. Hypocrisy permeated every syllable of the trap in this unanswerable conundrum. The obvious answer would be polyandry: polygyny had once been practised, as was said of Solomon. There was a curious expectation that an unmarried brother would marry a brother's wife, if he died leaving her childless. Here we have the revered number of seven brothers marrying the same woman in succession, not even the last leaving any issue. Jesus's reply is of the most signifiant importance: heaven is quite different from this world and this world's institutions, rules and customs have no relevance there. The implied instruction is to worry about the next world when one arrives in it and not before, as it is this world about which we need urgently to bother, not the next, following the parable of the lilies in all their glory. In effect, when he says in

v. 26 that God is the God of the living, Jesus is stating that we all are alive, even after we leave this world. It will probably help if we arrive there with as clean a bill of living as possible from when we were alive on earth.

Vv. 28-34 show how a scribal question, 'What is the first commandment of all?', elicited an all-encompassing summary of the law: 'Love God with all your might and your neighbour as yourself.' It echoes George Herbert's lines:

Teach me, my God and King,
In all things thee to see;
And what I do in anything
To do it as for thee.

We do not see God directly but we see God in the world around us, so we show our love for God by devoting our lives to looking after this world around us as well as we are able with God ever in mind. This is, in effect, all the law and the prophets.

V. 35 introduces a line of thought that has not, it might appear, been fully taken into account. Jesus shows that scripture contradicts the scribal interpretation which declares that God's anointed has to be a son of David. Jesus could be interpreted as saying, 'If I am messiah, I am more than just a descendant of David.'

V. 38 describes Jesus making fun of those who seek to inflate their sense of self-importance by occupying the most prominent and prized positions at public functions, pointing out that what one actually does is so much more important than any residual reputation.

Vv. 41-4, about the widow's two coins, are very important. What we do or give to help others is to be measured, not by relation to the size of the benefit conferred but by relation to the ability of the doer or the giver to help. If someone has little but gives as much as possible, that is better than one who gives a smaller proportion of much greater resources when more would have helped and could have been done or given.

Chapter 13 presents challenges. It is clear that eschatological interest was very prominent in the minds of many at that time and that Jesus, who regularly displayed such unprecedented understanding of every situation they encountered, may have been asked often about what he thought was going to happen. The Jews had come to realise that their political and military power were quite insufficient to free them from domination by others and were even less adequate for making them the most powerful nation of all, as they thought God's promises had destined them to be: they were God's chosen people after all, so they *had* to be top nation. Their own well-established ideas of how cataclysmic happenings in a manically depraved world were to introduce intervention from God, which would end with the Jews being above everyone else, seem to be catalogued in Jesus's response. This chapter certainly sets out a Jewish view of the future, but it must be less certain that it represents what Jesus actually believed and said, as what he taught was not only for the Jews but also for everyone else on earth, present and future. The writer may have given this particularly Jewish slant here to persuade his readers that he was fully aware of what was expected by the Jews so that his work would be accorded some respect by them.

This chapter seems to be something of a jumble of notions, not dissimilar to those occasions when Luke seems to muddle pieces of information up, as he seems to have done when he picked up Mark's description of the power of faith as being able to move mountains, which represent difficulties to the Jewish mind, while Luke (17:6) describes the power of faith as being sufficient to move 'sycamine' trees or bushes, which are less likely to be equated with the idea of difficulties: Luke has confused two separate items stemming from the teaching of Jesus.[19] A strong contributing factor to the confusion will have been the writer's mentally fusing the Old Testament vision of the 'Day of the Lord' with the second coming of Jesus.

The ambiguities may contain seemingly prescient ideas; we have the forewarning that the revenge of the Romans when totally frustrated by the intransigence of the Jews will result in the complete destruction of their Temple (v. 2); we have the warning about people claiming to be the true messengers or prophets of God in v. 22, trying to usurp the role of Jesus, and then recruiting people to believe in their false creeds, which seems fairly easily predictable and has never stopped happening; then there is the prophecy about the site of the Temple being desecrated, which was somewhat less easily predictable; there is reference to those ghastly regimes (v. 12) in which the culture is so pernicious that even children betray (inform on) one another and their parents, and parents inform on their children, leading to their deaths.

We start with an implied question, in v.1, exclaiming at the wonders of the Temple's magnificence, its construction with such enormous stones – apparently dwarfing the stones of Stonehenge – for which one may deduce the answer might have been post hoc, as the destruction of the Temple in 70 AD seems to be clearly in the mind of the writer; this may have been a later addition to an original version. One should bear in mind that Jesus would have been all too aware of the bigoted intransigence of the orthodox and highly influential religious authorities, which more or less guaranteed a clash with the Roman rulers, and that, as the seat of the problem was in adamantine religious inflexibility, the Temple, the centre-piece of the Judaic religion, would almost certainly be destroyed, in the hopes that, thereby, the Jewish will to resist would also be crushed. After the fall of Jerusalem to the army of Titus and the ensuing slaughter of almost unbelievable numbers, the heroic resistance to the Roman forces, at Masada (Metsada) in 73-4 AD, demonstrates with desperate clarity the lengths to which the Jewish spirit could drive these people.

In v. 3 the scene is set with Jesus, accompanied by Peter, Andrew, James and John who ask when the apocalypse will be. Alan Cole points out the interesting inclusion of Andrew, Peter's brother, and wonders why he was not mentioned as being with the group more often. Peter's fishing business was probably being kept going by Andrew, so he will have been unavailable much of the time. James and John, being the younger sons of an established and considerably larger business, will not have been missed by their family concerns.

Jesus starts (vv. 5 & 6) with the forecast that many impostors would come in his name, of whom they should beware. This seems to fit well with the wild proliferation of improbable faiths which have come into existence since then and which, often none too convincingly, claim divine inspiration as their source. Jesus makes this clear when he says in v. 6 that the false emissaries will say, "I am, *I am*", 'I Am' being a Jewish name for God. This might have been part of the explanation of Jesus referring to himself as 'Son of Man' on a number of occasions.

How strange, nevertheless, with reference to vv. 7-8, it would seem, that all the 'boxes were being ticked' in 2022: wars were being fought, while worse were threatened, in many regions; climate-change induced droughts afflicted some areas, resulting in famine, which was exacerbated by the war in Ukraine and wars elsewhere; false beliefs led to murderous acts of terrorism and to the existence of satanically driven governments, such as those in Iran and Afghanistan; there was an appalling amount of criminal activity, much associated with the distribution of illicit drugs. However, there seemed to be little mention of destructive winds and rising sea levels. Volcanic eruptions that often accompany earthquakes and the dangers of asteroid impacts, as one might expect, also escaped mention. Disease was not mentioned and that has been a terrible scourge in the past; for instance, the Black Death which killed an enormous proportion of the population in Europe in the 14th century, or the Plague which preceded the Great Fire of London in the 17th century. These were serious disasters.

There is a cautionary note as to timing, however: Jesus goes on to say (end v. 7), "The end is *still* to come", and (end v. 8), "These are (but) the *first* birth pangs of the new age." The forecasts that the followers of Jesus would suffer so terribly were almost certainly written after the persecutions had already begun – an even later addition? However, in v. 10 we see that his version of the new Judaism has to be preached to everyone in the world first.

The instruction (v.11) that, when challenged in

connection with matters of faith, they should put their trust in being given inspiration from God, by the Holy Spirit, would seem likely to have a genuine source.

There is a very interesting piece, at v. 14, where Jesus says (translation from the Oxford Study Bible), 'But when you see the "abomination of desolation" usurping a place which is not his, let the reader understand…'. Cole, p. 277, translates the object that desecrates as 'the idol that profanes' and the mosque on the site of the Temple represents very well such an idol. One might remember that the Muslim scripture, in trying to undermine Judaism and denigrate Christianity, asserts that Abraham was not a Jew but a Muslim[20], while it asserts that the one crucified was not Jesus but a likeness.[21] The Al Aqsa mosque, which, with its antecedents, has already, in 2022, been there for more than 1,300 years, would seem to be such a desecration in the eyes of Jews and Christians. The striking characteristic of this forecast is the resemblance, in its combination of precision and ambiguity, to the forecast in Isaiah 53:9 about the death of Jesus. Each, without the details of the event foretold to explain how it is to be applied, lacks real meaning; the moment, however, one has learnt about the actual event to which the prophecy applies the whole becomes clear, in the manner of Monet's Water Lilies in the Musée de l'Orangerie: as one backs away from a close-up view of the meaningless jumble of colours the lilies suddenly emerge into sight. This happens with these forecasts: the detail of the eventual outcome on each occasion brings apparent jumbles of the past prophecy into sharp, informing focus.

Vv. 15-20 contain terrible warnings about how urgent managing to escape will be; these would fit the Roman intervention in 70-74 AD very aptly, but must have general application, so unpredictable is the state of the world at this moment at the beginning of 2023. However, when we read that there are those who are the chosen of the Lord, we may suspect a very human interpretation: God loves everyone and everything.

In vv. 21 & 22 we have the warning about future preachers of false faiths repeated.

Vv. 24-37 seem a fantastical combination of the day of doom and the second coming of Jesus and we then learn, in apparent contradiction of vv. 7-10, that the end is nigh and that the present generation will live to see it all. Then, paradoxically, we are told in v. 32 that no one, except the Father, has any idea about when everything is going to happen. The chapter ends with the stern admonition always to be vigilant, which is not too different from 'And live this day as if thy last!' in the words of Bishop Ken in his hymn, 'Awake my soul, and with the sun', who went on to say, 'Redeem thy mis-spent time that's past': enjoy life helping others! The anthropomorphic vision in the writer of Mark's mind shows all too clearly that most of this chapter comes from his mind and not from what he might have learned about Jesus.

Chapter 14 introduces the last days of the ministry. We should, perhaps, remember that in John, when Jesus and his disciples cross the Kedron to gather in the garden of Gethsemane after supper, this wadi, which was a drain from the Temple, is described as being in heavy winter-style flow. Only the blood of slaughtered lambs would seem convincingly to explain this being a 'torrent' at that time of year. The number of lambs slaughtered was enormous and the ritual attending the disposal of the blood will have required a similarly demanding amount of time. The slaughtering will have had to begin much earlier than the originally stipulated hour. The Last Supper could thus have taken place on the day before Passover but, as it was to be their last supper together, it was probably felt to be equivalent to a Passover meal, so the ritual attending such a meal may well have been observed. The other interesting divergence is the placing of the prayers. John evidently does not take readily to the idea of Jesus praying to God since he is being presented as God, so he is portrayed as speaking his prayers publicly at the supper table, whereas the Synoptics have Jesus praying while the disciples sleep, after the supper, in the Garden of Gethsemane. We do not know what he was praying about, unless, as the Synoptic writers seem to think, it is about the terrible death he now knows he is to endure and for the people, including Judas, who are involved in carrying out this terrible atrocity.

First we are told, without explanation, that the scribes and Pharisees were trying to find reasons to have Jesus put to death; they wanted to avoid carrying this out during the very popularly attended Passover festival (v. 2), in case they might cause a riot thereby. Passover is only two days away, so this statement does not fit the actual situation, demonstrating the limited access to reliable information enjoyed by the writer. In fact, a good reason for having Jesus executed was already in their armoury: by undermining the authority of the scribal interpretation of the law, he was guilty of the capital offence of false teaching, in their eyes – the sorcery, involving telepathy and healing, was not, on its own, sufficient reason, although it was powerful evidence for the divine source of Jesus's work, which will have given rise to very considerable concern among them all.

In v. 3 we have the explanation that they are now in Bethany, one of the official places for people to stay for the Passover, as there was never enough room in Jerusalem for everybody who wanted to attend this centrally important feast. Here, Jesus is anointed by a lady, who is fully identified as Mary, the sister of Martha and Lazarus, only in John (12:3). Luke (7:36-50), who gives the most elaborate account, places this unexpectedly in the house of a Pharisee called Simon and relatively early in the ministry, without stating that Jesus saw this as an anointing for his burial, as did the writers of the other three Gospels. Luke is almost certainly correct to say it was Jesus's feet that received the attention from a sinner, as anointing the head conferred honour on the anointer as well as on the anointed; he may well have been right to say that the unspecified ointment was in an alabaster flask, as did Mark, who also said it was genuine nard (also 'spikenard') which came from India and that she broke the flask because the recipient was so special. He is unlikely to have been right as to some of the other details he gives; it seems that the woman was not even an invited guest. Mark, who is copied by Matthew (26:6-7), says that this took place in the house of Simon the Leper (perhaps representing Lazarus, or Lazarus's father, as John says) and again that it was the head of Jesus that was anointed by a woman who came and was not said to be a guest. Matthew does not specify the ointment, he just says it was very expensive and that it was the disciples in general who complained about the waste. According to John, Martha was serving, so it would have been her house, as Professor William Barclay points out in his commentary on John (Edinburgh, 1975, vol. 2, p. 109). The discrepancies and the lack of detailed precision in the Synoptics suggest that the story is authentic and that the trustworthy version is to be found in John.

It is at this juncture in v. 10 that Mark places the departure of Judas to the Chief Priests, to arrange his betrayal, as does Matthew (26:14), whereas Luke places it a little before the Last Supper. John's account, which does not tell us when Judas actually decided to betray Jesus, is rather more compelling, because of the flawless air of authenticity that permeates the whole narration.

V. 12 introduces a somewhat elaborate and mysterious account of how two unnamed disciples would encounter a water carrier who would lead them into the right house for the disciples to prepare supper. The upper room is likely to have been accessible by an outside stairway and will have had many purposes, such as a storeroom or guest-room, for the householder. Luke has the same account but with the extra convincing detail that it was Peter and John, the apparently inseparable pair, who were to sort out the house and meal; it may have been John's family-owned house. Matthew has a more elaborate and so less plausible narrative. The absence of any seemingly contrived or otherwise implausible complications in John's straightforward account makes that one sound right. A note on p. 289 in Cole's commentary makes a very suggestive point: 'John, as often, seems to be deliberately writing, probably at a later date, to correct an unconscious *misunderstanding* of [for this read *misinformation* in] the earlier accounts.' The writer, provided it was John the Elder, writer of the three letters in his name, was exercising his superior knowledge, as he demonstrated in his dismissal of the chronology in Mark, which had informed, in turn, the chronology in the other two Synoptics. It is very interesting that every narrative points out or indicates that the Passover lambs were being slaughtered that day. If they were being slaughtered for the next day, the next day was Passover. The official programme for the slaughter dictated that the slaughter was to begin at either 2 or 3 in the afternoon of the day of Passover. However, as has been pointed out earlier, with the ritual passing of the cups holding the blood of the slaughtered lambs between priests, when the number of lambs to be slaughtered was in excess of 200,000, the ceremonial slaughtering will have had to start so much earlier that the evening of the previous day would seem the more likely start for the ceremony. For the Jews, as the 'day' started with sunset, this was not so obviously a problem. There would not be any breach of the law in that there would be sacrifice in progress at the stipulated times, although, because of the pressure of numbers the process would have had to start much earlier; the scribes would have worked out some legal circumvention to allow what was a departure from the original requirements, although, very naturally, such 'shady evasion' was not chronicled anywhere.

V.17 starts with the description of Jesus coming to the house with the twelve; this contrasts with the account in John which makes no mention of how Jesus and those with him came to be at a supper table. Had the writer of John been compiling his account on his own he would probably have made some statement about their coming into the house, or at least, taking up their positions at the table, but, with the witness there and following his recital of his memories, he just followed what he was hearing and so left this part out; the presence and stream of information coming from the witness blocked out any consciousness of this literary lacuna in his narrative. This almost guarantees that what we learn from John is right.

V. 18 states that Jesus declared that one of those at supper with him was going to betray him. This is recounted in all four Gospels; it contributes nothing to the image which the writers wanted to convey so it is more or less certain to be accurate, just as the betrayer will be the one named also. Nevertheless, it would seem very likely that they all would have known, from the way Jesus made the declaration, that the betrayal was going to be a deliberate act; none of them would have been asking of one another, as in v. 19, "Surely it is not I?". This demonstrates how the writer tried to fill perceived gaps and the relative naivety of his understanding, while dismay would have been a better description of their feelings than grief: he was not a prototype novelist. The claim that it would have been better for that man (the betrayer) not to have been born in v. 21 shows even more clearly that the writer knew very little of the real character of Jesus: he understood every human failing, while the thinking that led Judas to betray Jesus was almost certainly very complicated. Jesus would have understood it all; he will have known whether Judas was trying to force his hand, to make God come to his rescue, or trying to find out if Jesus really was divine – for he will have thought that God was bound to defend his own. A 'decision' to turn against Jesus for some personal grudge is not probable because Jesus was so astute in the way he managed people. Curiously, any great need for a betrayer to enable the religious authorities to find and arrest Jesus is unlikely, so the general line of the story is almost certainly authentic. One might bear in mind that Judas is not alone in having a second name attached to his first: there is Simon bar Jonah for Peter, as well as Simon the Cananean in Mark's list of the disciples and Simon the Zealot; perhaps Judas was a nationalist too and, thinking Jesus was letting the side down by not being militant, betrayed him because of that. There is the curiosity that the name Iscariot has spelling and sound connections with the Latin word 'sicarius' (e.g *sicariot*) which means 'assassin' from the word for a dagger. Apparently, those Jewish zealots who were prepared to murder in their cause were called 'sicarii'. Such changes in spelling are replicated in the way the Latin word for yesterday, or the day before today, 'heri', is now 'hier' in French.[22]

In v. 22 we have the institution of the taking of bread and wine in memory of Jesus. This giving of bread and wine at Passover by the head of the family, the Kiddush, is not mentioned in John, although it fits with earlier parabolic commands there. The idea, however, that it should be a memorial to Jesus, is so different from what one might expect that it is almost certainly a correct record. On the other hand, when one reads in v. 25 that Jesus will not drink of the fruit of the vine until that day he drinks it new in the kingdom of God, we may be sure that this kingdom is here on earth and not in heaven, as heaven is God's domain, where all is so different from anything on earth that there is no comparison which can make any sense. Somehow, when the new world, which is envisaged in Isaiah, comes into being, Jesus will be with all who are there when they 'drink together'.

There is an arresting connection with Zechariah chapter 12:2: 'I am about to make Jerusalem an intoxicating cup for all.' Jesus was instituting a new one-way covenant with God's unconditional love, as is explained by Barclay, p. 357 of his commentary. The 'mountain of the Lord's house' in Isaiah 2:2 (and also Micah 4:1), 'mountain of the Lord' in v. 3 (Micah 4:2) and 'holy mountain' (Isaiah 11:9), where only goodwill will reign, represent Judaism, as does Zechariah's Jerusalem which is to be a cup for everyone.[23] The idea that all the nations of the earth will be marshalled to attack Jerusalem, might be likened to the multiplicity of competing faiths that are now gathering on every side and seem intent on enticing people away from what is pictured in Zechariah and Isaiah. Jesus's witness, together with the prophecies in Isaiah, Micah and Zechariah predict that the God of the Jews will eventually be the God of us all, wherever we may be. That will be the golden age of heaven on earth.

Zechariah 12:10: 'When they look on me, on him whom they have pierced', evokes an interesting commentary in the Oxford Study Bible on p. 614. The scene of people beholding the death of a martyr and being moved by a spirit of grace is the introduction, with concern expressed as to how human guilt is to be removed. Here we remember 'Grace and truth came by Jesus Christ', as John wrote in 1:17. The one who is pierced is God – so is Jesus for many people – and the paradox and ambiguity identified here may seem difficult to explain at first, but not so difficult when these words are seen as a prophecy of crucified Jesus's side being pierced by a Roman soldier's spear. One might remember that Jesus is God's direct and directed agent and so, in that way, God in human form.

The singing of a hymn in v. 26 is mentioned also in Matthew, but not in Luke or John. We have next in vv. 27-8 the reference, 'I will strike the shepherd and the sheep will be scattered', which must be to Zechariah 13:7, where it is God who will strike the shepherd and not a man and where God will turn against the lambs, but then: 'It will happen throughout the land that two thirds of the people will be struck down and die, while one third of them will be left...I shall refine them...I shall say "These are my people" and they will say "The Lord is my God."'The twist at the end might make it all relevant. The adult male disciples were indeed scattered when they lost their shepherd on the cross.

In vv. 29-31 we have Peter's claiming that he will never deny knowing Jesus and Jesus saying that he would do that before the double cockcrow signal. The other disciples declared the same too, but they were not brave enough to follow Jesus to the houses of Annas and Caiaphas. None of them had imagined the pressures that were to build up against them when they made their declarations of loyalty. Of course, Peter had to deny knowing Jesus in the circumstances, as he would otherwise have been eliminated before he could have done anything else, particularly as he had just tried to kill the High Priest's agent.

In v. 32 we read, "into a place named 'Gethsemane'", which makes a very interesting comparison with what appears in John. In John the detail has all the hallmarks of an eyewitness account: there they cross a normally dry drain from the Temple, which is a streaming torrent at the moment of crossing, and enter a garden; the name is not important enough to have been given there; John, the son of Zebedee, knows exactly where they went while Mark shows clearly that he does not know the scene nearly as intimately as the witness for John. John's account is firsthand and Mark's thirdhand.

From v. 32 on we have the story of Jesus leaving the

main body of the disciples with the customary three, Peter, James and John, and then the harrowing account of Jesus's distress and his later praying when faced with the horrors that are to ensue. The three are described as sleeping and then being awakened by Jesus three times. There is no witness for what Jesus prayed, so it must be the conjecture of the writer, while there is no obvious reason for Jesus singling out and taking the traditional three and then leaving them after that to move a little further on. We may be sure that there was turmoil in Jesus's mind, but it would seem likely that the writer fashioned his version to fill a gap. When we have the scene of the arrest by the agents of the religious authorities, we may contrast the scene in Mark with John's, where there have been no special praying sessions on the part of Jesus and where Judas, although he is accompanying the arresting band, takes no part in the actual betrayal – the witness may have expunged that repulsive memory from his mind. In John it is Jesus who 'betrays' himself. Judas has merely led the band to the right place, which makes good sense. However, the horror of a betraying kiss seems plausible, so strange for us is the idea.

Next we have (v. 47) a bystander, who must be Peter, incompetently trying to kill the High Priest's agent. We may be sure that this happened as it does not confer credit on anyone. However, although not mentioned in Mark, Jesus's instruction to Peter to sheathe his sword, attested by Matthew, Luke and John, enables us to understand that Jesus abhorred violence; we therefore know that anyone who uses violence in the name of Jesus, or God, is guilty of an appalling failure to understand his teaching. Of some importance is the prohibition of carrying swords on the day of Passover, which supports the contention that the last supper was not an actual Passover meal.

When the armed band is upbraided by Jesus in v. 48 for coming to arrest him with swords (further evidence that this not Passover itself) and cudgels he makes it evident that he rejects any form of violence, while he points out that his teaching in the Temple which has been 'available' to everyone has made his position on this clear. He refers again to the scripture quoted in 14:27.

In vv. 51-2 we have the surprising inclusion of the story of the young man whom the authorities wanted to seize. He managed to escape, but not with his clothing. Clearly he was someone on a 'wanted list' and there is no known reason for thinking that the writer, or the source for the material, possessed such a list; in addition, the lack of definitive detail in his account would suggest that the writer of the Gospel, or, rather, the source, was not present at the arrest anyway. John's Gospel *does* give another one on the authorities' wanted list, Lazarus, as it was his apparent resuscitation from the dead that so worried them. If the probably young Lazarus had been wearing only his burial cloth as a special memento, this will explain how he was singled out from the rest of the crowd so easily and sought with such determination. The writer of the Gospel will probably have known the name but 'withheld' it because the man was still alive. How or why this story was interpolated is difficult to explain, unless it was added so as to endow the account with authenticity. The information will have come from Peter, who will have been pleased to note that someone else was running away when he was not, and he would certainly have wanted others to know this.

Before we read about the trial, we might do well to take into account what Professor Sanders says on p. 297 of his book, 'Jesus and Judaism', of the Synoptic Gospel accounts of the hearings and trial: "The exchanges between the high priest and Jesus in the synoptic accounts, especially in Matthew and Mark, do not carry conviction." Sanders says on p. 67 of his book, 'The Historical Figure of Jesus': "In terms of *intrinsic probability,* the Johannine trial scene is much more likely than that of the Synoptics." A useful way in which to assess the account follows.

Jesus is then taken to the house of Caiaphas in v. 53, which information will have come from Peter. The writer of John says they went to the house of Annas first, which is probably right, but that writer had got the wrong end of the stick, as to where the main religious trial took place, when he was questioning the witness about the events of that evening. He mistakenly thought that it was in the house of Annas that the reported 'trial' had taken place. The actual details in John's account make it plain that the reported trial took place in the house of the then High Priest, not that of Annas as the writer had been led to believe. All the same, Annas, the father-in-law of Caiaphas, though he may have been High Priest no longer, still wielded enormous influence; according to Barclay (John, vol. 2, p. 225), his toxic character and unmerited good fortune were renowned. A preliminary visit to his house, prior to the main hearing before the religious authorities in the house of Caiaphas, sounds very likely.

V. 54, Jesus is followed by Peter and John, which is corroborated by John, while Peter stayed in the courtyard to warm himself at a fire, which was described in a little more detail by John. The description in John about the fire inside the courtyard contains more circumstantial detail, indicating that the report in Mark is further down the chain of information, so it is not surprising that Mark's account of the trial seems to be from his deductions and without any firsthand input from a witness being evident. In addition, there is no explanation in Mark as to how Peter might have been admitted into the courtyard in the first place.

V. 55 states that the assembled 'council' tried to find evidence. This seems somewhat strange as there is likely to have been evidence in their minds already, otherwise such a trial would seem improbable. If one accepts that the accounts of the trials in John are almost certainly correct, as is argued on pp. 91-99 in 'Where is the Evidence?' (Matador, 2022), one can see how inadequate are the accounts in the Synoptic Gospels. Peter in the courtyard is unlikely to have heard much or learned more and so will not have provided much information about the actual trial to his audiences when he was spreading the message.

In vv. 57-8 we have a useful contribution: 'Some stood up and gave false evidence against him to this effect: we heard him say, "I will pull down this temple made with human hands, and in three days I will build another, not made with hands."' This is a very significant entry. It is not, if we are to trust the witness based account in John[24], wholly false, while the confused detail shows that it is based on proper information which has become distorted during transmission. The original version is to be found in John 2:18-21, after the cleansing of the Temple. This provides a very telling insight into the makeup of the information which the writers of the Gospels used and how what they deduced came to be true and false at the same time. It also tells us how they tried to fill in the gaps which they thought needed to be filled. Indeed, this anomaly in Mark's account is one of the clearest pieces of evidence that can be found to show exactly how we should assess the information provided by the writers of the Gospels.

Unfortunately, John's Gospel does not provide much information about what was actually said during the trial in the house of Caiaphas, although it is quite likely that more happened there than is told in that Gospel. Although it is not possible to dismiss the account that follows in vv. 60-4 in Mark, this cannot be relied on as being factual. This part of the account may actually have occurred in the trial before Pilate. However, once again, in v. 65, we have behaviour that is far more likely to have happened, if it took place as related, at or even after the trial before Pilate.

In v. 66 we have the first of Peter's denials that he knew Jesus. The absence of plausible context illustrates the writer's lack of access to firsthand information. There is no indication as to why the girl should have concluded he knew Jesus, whereas in John, when Peter has just been admitted to the courtyard because of the intercession of a lad who was known to associate with Jesus, the connection is obvious, not just the Galilean accent, which, on its own, would not have been enough. With the second cockcrow signal, Peter is described as weeping, a useful circumstantial detail perhaps.

The night-time part of the trial now ends, as all the Gospel stories agree, and action is transferred to the prefect's domain. Once again, the only male witness to the course of events was the very young witness to John's account, so only in that narrative may we confidently place trust. This account is extraordinary.

First Pilate comes out of his headquarters to ask the band of Jews who have brought Jesus what the accusation might be. These Jews have stayed outside to avoid ritual defilement as the Passover celebrations are to take place that evening, which makes it clear that this meeting is a last minute arrangement, as in normal circumstances Pilate would have been informed about everything in advance. They reply that they would not have brought Jesus there if he had not done wrong, which is not an answer. It is so completely true to life that it could not, by any stretch of the imagination, have been invented by the writer. We then have the entirely predictable instruction from Pilate that they should deal with the matter themselves, which fits his character and any run of events one might anticipate.

However, the religious authorities point out that they do not have the legal power to execute anyone. Whereupon Pilate goes back into the praetorium to question Jesus further. Here, far more realistically than in the Synoptic accounts, Pilate asks, obviously after picking up an extra piece of information at some time, which is not accounted for by the witness, 'So are you the king of the Jews then?' Jesus's not answering the question but asking whether Pilate had been put up to ask this or decided to ask of his own accord, is further proof that this is a true record of all that is related. Pilate's evasion of the true answer, that he had indeed been advised by the authorities that this was their charge against Jesus, demonstrates the reliability of this account. His 'Am I a Jew?', which will have been spat out with unconcealed contempt, is yet another detail of inescapable authenticity. We next have the further claim that Jesus had been brought before Pilate by the authorities and *people*, which was not the case: it was only the religious authorities who were responsible for all this, but they will have implied or alleged that the majority opinion supported their point of view. Pilate asked what Jesus had done wrong. This time there is clearly a gap in the testimony of the witness, as Jesus answers the previous question by admitting that he is a king of the Jews but not in this world. There follows the apparently strange claim that if he were an earthly king his supporters would be there fighting to save him from the Jews, *but they had all run away.* Pilate, needing to establish grounds for imposing a death penalty, asks, 'So you are really a king?', to which Jesus assents adding that he had been born for this purpose, to bear witness to the truth. Pilate's question about what truth is, goes unanswered. Instead, Pilate tries to escape having to impose the death penalty by telling the authorities, absolutely correctly, that there is no charge against Jesus that can be substantiated – his claim to kingship is not of this world. We are then given the same account in every Gospel about Pilate trying to have Jesus released but the hand-picked crowd choosing Barabbas instead; he was the one who really was guilty, as far as we can tell, of trying to overthrow the rule of the Roman state.

According to John's account Jesus is now scourged and the soldiers crown and robe Jesus in purple, mocking him with 'Hail, king of the Jews!' and slapping him. Pilate then declares that he has found no fault in Jesus and that he is bringing him out to them; as he does so he declares, 'Ecce homo!' Jesus comes out wearing the crown and robed in purple. The chief priests and officers then shout out that Jesus should be crucified, whereupon Pilate exclaims, 'You take and crucify him yourselves because I have not found him guilty of any crime.' To this the 'Jews' reply that they have a law that anyone should die who has set himself up as a son of God – which charge Jesus has already refuted in John 10:34-6, where Jesus refers to Psalm 82:6. The text then says that Pilate was afraid, though it was almost certainly not fear but intensely irritated frustration on his part at having to deal with such small-minded intransigence. Here there is an aporia, which fits the disjointed interrogation that lay behind the writing of the Gospel, as Pilate is said to go back into the praetorium to question Jesus further when there has been no mention of Jesus being taken back into it. The question now put is indubitably from an acute memory of what actually transpired: 'Where are you from?', as no such novelistic invention could possibly have been in the writer's mental resources. This is astonishingly true to life. This is the moment when

Jesus genuinely decides not to answer. Next comes the interchange in which Pilate points out that Jesus should answer as he (Pilate) has the authority to release him or have him crucified. We have the typical reply – surely genuine – 'You would have no authority over me if it had not been granted from above; the one who handed me over to you is the one who is guilty of the greater sin.' Pilate now knows with absolute certainty that Jesus is not the fantasy-obsessed half-wit he may originally have imagined.

What follows is again beyond the inventive powers of the writer: Pilate wanted to release Jesus but the Jewish authorities retorted that, were he to do so, he would be no friend of Caesar's. Pilate now brings Jesus out again and sits on a raised pavement (Gabbatha). We now have the extraordinary interchange which Pilate begins with, 'See your king!' The authorities answer with 'Take him away and crucify him!' Pilate asks, 'Shall I crucify your king?' Whereupon they reply, 'We have no king but Caesar!' This is a complete abnegation of the required loyalty to their God before all others. Their presentation of the matter is tantamount to evidence that Jesus has to be crucified on the grounds of the implication that he is guilty of treason. Jesus is handed over to be crucified. Wherever Mark's account differs from that in John, it is John's that is to be preferred.

Mark relates in v. 15 that Pilate wanted to please the crowd; although there would be truth in that, the real reason was to keep the peace, the all-important Pax Romana, as is implied in the Oxford Commentary, p. 919. However, if there is an omission in John's account, such as the detail in v. 21 that Simon from Cyrene (in Africa), described as the father of Alexander and Rufus[25], was made by the Roman soldiery to 'volunteer' to carry the transom of the cross for Jesus, we may allow that this, particularly as it is a piece of unusual circumstantial detail, must have been missed by the witness for John's Gospel. It may have been an early example of recorded racial discrimination, as Simon was probably very dark-skinned. The witness may have been held up by the crowds at the time, or have broken down with grief. The Via Dolorosa may have been half a mile long, but it may well have been densely packed with people too.[26] All we may be sure of is that the witness was present at the crucifixion.

If there is any dislocation in the chronology in John's account it will be remembered that, as the witness was the disciple who loved Jesus most, the grief occasioned in remembering this terrible time might have interfered with his ability to communicate exactly the right order of events to the writer; we might, for instance, have the scourging placed at the wrong moment in John, as asking Jesus back for further questioning after scourging would seem less likely, so murderously painful will have been the experience. However, Mark and Matthew also put the scourging before a return into the praetorium, while

Luke has Pilate proposing, but not specifically carrying out, the scourging. However, the further questioning in John seems incontrovertibly authentic.

Mark, v. 23, states that Jesus was offered drugged wine before he was crucified, which he refused, but in John, Jesus actually said, when he had been on the cross for some time, that he thirsted and John implies that he must have sucked from a sponge soaked in vinegar on the end of a hyssop reed, as his final act before death. Mark should not be relied on here, although v. 36 may indicate a contradiction of sorts.

Jesus is crucified with two brigands (v. 27); the soldiers, unnumbered by Mark, *dice* in v. 24 for Jesus's garments – in John the four soldiers *cast lots* only for the single garment left over after the initial sharing out of the presumed four other items, which is circumstantial authentication of the account in John. In those days lots were cast by putting suitably inscribed shards, pieces of broken pottery, into a helmet and shaking it until one of the shards flew out. The time given in v. 25 was nine o'clock in the morning. Luke does not mention any inscription on the cross, but Mark, and then Matthew following him, have: 'Jesus, king of the Jews'. The extra detail in John came, presumably, from the witness, who, although illiterate, would have had enough intelligence, understanding and curiosity to ask questions or work out exactly what was there. John has not only: 'Jesus of Nazareth, king of the Jews', but also that it was written in Hebrew, Latin and Greek. This emphasises that Pilate was far more than usually interested in the affair. John adds too that the authorities requested that it should be explained on the inscription that it was Jesus who claimed to be king, as they did not like the implication that the Roman administration considered him their king. We have the remarkable riposte from Pilate: 'What I have written, I have written.' No literary invention may be imagined there, while the witness will have been so interested that he will have made sure that he knew exactly what Pilate's reply had been. The circumstantial detail in John confirms that this is the preferred account, the one that is likely to be correct, while it is interesting to note that the Synoptic writers seem to want to distance Jesus from Nazareth: perhaps they want Jesus to be thought of as coming from Bethlehem.

There is unanimity that two criminals were crucified with him, one on either side. The derisive mockery in v. 31, such as 'He saved others but he cannot save himself', as detailed in Mark, and followed by Matthew and Luke, may well have occurred, but either the witness to John had expunged it from his memory or the writer felt it inappropriate. The extra details in Mark: that there was darkness for three hours (v. 33); that, after Jesus had uttered a loud cry before his death, the curtain in the Temple was torn in two from top to bottom (v. 38); that a centurion then said (v. 39) he was a son of God, may all be symbolically true, but there was, almost certainly, no firsthand witness to attest to the veracity of these events. The cry (v. 34) attributed to Jesus, 'Eloi, Eloi lama sabachthani?' ('My God, my God, why hast thou forsaken me?') is predictably absent from John but is, because it does not fit the picture which Gospel writers want to present, very likely to be right, although the story will have come through a chain of several people first. It is possible, too, that people said, 'Let us see if Elijah *does* come to take him down.' In v. 36 someone offers sour wine (vinegar) soaked in a sponge on the end of a stick, not on hyssop as in John, but we are not told that Jesus 'drank' anything. As was suggested in 'Where is the Evidence?', p. 117, God may have taken away Jesus's feeling that God was there with him at that moment, to hasten the onset of death and shorten the period of intense pain and suffering; the resulting 'broken heart' may explain, perhaps, the blood and water flowing from the wound in Jesus's side which was vividly remembered by the witness to John.

However, the idea that a number of women watched from a distance is strong evidence that none of Mark's informants was there at the time. We may be sure, for instance, that Mary, mother of Jesus, was there, close by and not at a distance, when Jesus was crucified, and that it was likely that others also were close by.

There is totally convincing unanimity that the rich Joseph of Arimathea (v. 43) organised the taking down of Jesus's body and had it placed in his new and hitherto unused tomb. The surprise attributed to Pilate (v. 44) that Jesus had died so soon fits well with the way events must have occurred. Mark says that Joseph bought some linen (v. 46) in which to wrap the body but does not indicate that there was a separate piece for the head. Mark also states that Mary from Magdala and Mary, the mother of Jesus, were there at the entombment (v. 47), which would seem almost certainly correct, as they knew exactly where to go on the Sunday after that Passover sabbath, even if this time Mary Magdalen may have gone on her own.

Chapter 16 begins with the arrival at the tomb of Mary of Magdala and Mary, the mother of *James and Salome.* This is very interesting as there is likely to be confusion in this description. Salome may have been the name of the wife of Zebedee, the mother of James and John ('the beloved disciple') but Mark explains nothing of this, which suggests he has come across a convincing tradition which had been mangled during transmission. It seems that the witness to John's Gospel had learnt about only Mary of Magdala visiting the empty tomb that morning, while it would be likely that she had company on her journey there, so as to be safer. Mark's account thus commands some respect, although establishing with any certainty who this companion may have been, might seem a little more challenging.

The suggestion that the two ladies were wondering

(v. 3) who would roll away the stone is almost certainly conjecture, but probably right all the same. The remaining part of the writer's imagined picture is far less convincing and we should return to the account in John for a more likely scenario. Mark's vision of a young man – divine emissary – explaining the situation does not ring true. In John no one was needed to tell Mary of Magdala to run to tell Peter and John, while it would seem very unlikely that the two were so afraid (v. 8) that they told no one. Frightened people, particularly ladies, prefer supporting company to isolation.

The last part, vv.7-20, which seems to be an ill-fitting addition from another pen, is quite clearly conjecture built up from known traditions in the stories of others. Here the new writer follows, in his first episode, the outline in John, but in his account Mary from Magdala tells unnamed disciples what she has discovered. The disbelief, though general here, fits the account of 'Doubting Thomas' in John, while v. 12 fits Luke's account of the journey to Emmaus. Most interestingly, it is in this verse that Jesus is described as appearing in another form: this new writer understood very well that the risen Jesus was quite different from what he had been in his former bodily existence. We have next the idea that Jesus appeared to the 'Twelve' (v. 14) when they were at table to upbraid them for disbelief. This is an amalgam of the first appearance to the male disciples in John and the implied upbraiding of Peter in John 21:15-17, where it is Peter alone who is specially instructed to start spreading Jesus's message. The anthropomorphic ascent of Jesus into heaven might be almost taken from Acts 1:9-10.

We may not know how Mark's writer really finished this Gospel, but with John's account to guide us it does not matter too much. However, in all this one might remember that there were about one and a half days between Jesus's death on the cross and his appearance to Mary and that the disappearance of his body might have been even sooner, as the tomb was not visited on the sabbath.

SIX

—

Jesus was born into a joiner-builder family, to a mother named Mary, with a father named Joseph. He had brothers and sisters. Joseph may have died early on, so Jesus may have been the principal worker in the family business for some years before he began his ministry. The evidence suggests that he had almost preternatural telepathic and healing powers, while he also possessed considerable skills in influencing people. When he realised how unusual was his extraordinary array of talents, he spent a significant number of days (forty was not normally used specifically) in an unpopulated area, thinking about how he should use his gifts so as to benefit the ordinary people of the land. This was probably before the baptism.

During this period of meditation he chanced upon John the Baptist and something induced him to be baptised in the Jordan along with others. Very soon after this he was chosen by, or chose, the disciples, John, Andrew, Simon, Philip and Nathanael, after which he undertook his ministry, which lasted for something over two years.

He had decided, in effect, to give up a 'good job' and go off preaching a new way of thinking about God. This is unlikely to have been regarded as completely normal by the family or any one else. He was about thirty years old when he was baptised by John the Baptist, although there is an estimate for late forties.[27] Early on he 'cleansed' the Temple, which act might have persuaded other members of his family to try to take him out of public life. The cleansing appears to have persuaded the religious authorities that he was possessed by a demon, as they would have dealt with him much sooner had this not been so. However, an important reason for the 'violent' conduct of Jesus on this occasion was his determination to condemn publicly the ruthless financial exploitation of the poor, as well as everyone else, by the Temple authorities. Jesus's subsequent conduct and almost unparalleled command of any subject, during discussion, argument and preaching, throughout his subsequent ministry, will have made Caiaphas realise that Jesus was not mentally deranged, as he had thought originally, when he first learnt about the cleansing of the temple.

Jesus's teaching was probably concerned to an

important extent with exposing as wrong the exaggerated burden of the law on life in general; everyone was a slave to it and, thereby, to the scribes. He was therefore seen as a champion of ordinary people. Those who vaunted their meticulous attention to every detail of legal requirement in the endless scribal lists were shown to be putting their faith, quite pointlessly, in their own vain, self-glorious beliefs. As a result, his teaching was described as false by the authorities and regarded as a threat to their control. However, Jesus was not trying to start a new religion; he was just clearing away the over-grown jungle of shackling intricacies of scribal interpretation of the law, while he remained loyal to Judaism.

He used wonderfully apposite and remarkably arresting parables to illustrate what he was teaching. The extent of his telepathic and healing powers appeared to be miraculous and attracted a strong and widespread belief that his authority was from God. He seems to have possessed an extensive knowledge of scripture, very astute diplomatic skills, a lively sense of fun, a sharp wit, the penetrating ability to see rapidly the heart of any problem with which he was confronted, while having an acute eye for any weakness in an opponent's argument. He was equipped with this wide-ranging intellectual command, even though he had previously been just an artisan, who would not have been expected to have either such learning or such understanding.

Particularly remarkable was his ability to stay completely fearless and mentally composed when threatened with the most painful death imaginable. Just as remarkable were his powers, not only to cure mental disorders and heal other diseases, but also to recognise that some moribund people were in comas and not actually dead, as others, including the writers of the Gospels, thought, as well as to resuscitate them. No wonder it may have been he who was described as guilty of sorcery in the Babylonian Talmud!

The religious authorities, when they perceived that Jesus's influence was becoming dangerously powerful from their point of view, decided, with the prompting of Caiaphas, the High Priest, to have Jesus executed by the Roman administration, on the grounds that he was a threat to peace and stability. His followers were not thought to be sufficiently numerous, motivated or powerful enough to be a problem, while it was believed that the ignominious death of the leader would set so strong a seal of official disapproval on the venture and instil such fear that nothing from it would survive. Indeed, following the crucifixion, the band of disciples did initially keep themselves well out of the public eye when they gathered together.

There was a last supper, at Passover, or on the day before, with important members of a group termed 'disciples' or 'apostles', during which one of them – it later turned out to be Judas, son of Simon Iscariot – was declared by Jesus as going to betray him. At this supper Jesus instituted a rite of taking bread and sharing wine from a communal cup, representing his body and blood, to be performed by followers in his memory; he forecast that Simon, nicknamed 'Peter' (Rock) in jest, because he was so impulsive, would deny he knew Jesus three times before the early morning cockcrow signal. Peter did indeed, on three occasions, deny he knew Jesus before that signal, while Jesus was being heard by an ad hoc session of a High Priest court, late at night in the High Priest's house. Peter was absolutely right to deny he knew Jesus, as to have done so would have led to his being eliminated before he could do anything to spread the message of Jesus: he had just tried to kill the High Priest's agent. This was followed by an early morning hearing outside the prefect's building, presided over by Pontius Pilate. Here it was decided he should be crucified. We may be sure that the authorities would not have executed the wrong person by mistake as he was so famous that they will have known exactly what he looked like. After all, they had had Judas to lead them to the right man…or was Judas having the last laugh? Very doubtful!

On the occasion of his arrest Jesus made it absolutely clear that he abjured any personal violence – when he cleansed the Temple, his 'violence' had been directed against the means and not the people. His teaching was not to be defended by the sword and certainly not prosecuted by it. Neither the Crusades nor the Spanish Inquisition would have been sanctioned by him. The execution and torture of those deemed to be heretics or pagans would have been utterly condemned. He was a man of love and peace; disputes were to be resolved by reason and amicable argument alone.

After being crucified, Jesus somehow appeared 'out of thin air', in an often initially unrecognised form, to a number of his devoted followers and to his presumed to be previously overtly 'unbelieving' brother, James, who may have entertained a sneaking admiration for Jesus's new thinking which he had hidden from the rest of the family. The extensive number of people who were prepared to suffer torture and death for this belief in the continuing existence of Jesus demonstrates that they considered it to be of supreme importance and its truth quite beyond question. Immediately after the crucifixion there had been a lull, but suddenly there was a resurgence which can be satisfactorily explained only by something such as the reappearance of Jesus following his death on the cross. We may be sure, then, that there was a 'resurrection', but we may be just as sure that it was almost certainly not one that was 'bodily'.

EPILOGUE

—

If what has been argued here is right, we are left with accepting first, that there is only one true God, about whom we cannot know anything except that God exists, similar to the Jews when they gave God the name 'I Am', and secondly, what we have learnt from Jesus: that God loves his creation. Jesus, as God's specially directed agent, is the nearest representation of God that we may conceive, but he is not God, just as the Holy Sprit, or Breath of God, is not. Nevertheless, some of us may be able to feel, at least some of the time, that, in some indefinable way, God and Jesus are reassuringly with us; this may be one of the functions of the Holy Spirit, the life-giving breath of God. We know also that Jesus appeared to a special set of people after the crucifixion in some form and that there have been instances since that time when individual people felt that Jesus was appearing, somehow, to them.

We also accept that Jesus was born into a reasonably well-to-do family, and had exceptional endowments: a probably unprecedented combination of telepathic understanding, healing powers, powers to influence, an all-pervading sense of humour and an almost overpowering concern for all the oppressed among his fellowmen, children and women in particular. His coming onto the scene at this time is attributed to God's intervention in John 18:37, where Jesus answered Pilate's question: '*To this end I have been born,* and *for this I have come into the world,* to bear witness to the truth.' It is true that this might be embellishment from the pen of the writer, but it is as good as true, whether it is an addition from the pen of the writer or not. God used these exceptional endowments when he took over directing Jesus at the baptism, to spread the new message about how we should think about God and conduct our lives. So, if we are to demonstrate love for our creator, about whom we can, by definition, know nothing with certainty – apart from the two things, creation and love – we can do this only by loving and caring for God's creation, which is what the writer of John's Gospel emphasised with calculated repetition in his last chapters: when we love and care for everyone and everything around us, including the rest of the world, indeed the universe, and all that is in it, as well as we can, we are demonstrating our love for God.

NOTES

1

The Gospel of John, from a literary perspective; C.S. Lewis: 'In what is already a very old commentary I read that the Fourth Gospel is regarded by one school as a 'spiritual romance', 'a poem not a history', to be judged by the same canons as Nathan's parable, the Book of Jonah, *Paradise Lost* 'or, more exactly, *Pilgrim's Progress*'. After a man has said that, why need one attend to anything else he says about any book in the world? Note that he regards *Pilgrim's Progress*, a story which professes to be a dream and flaunts its allegorical nature by every single proper name it uses, as the closest parallel. Note that the whole epic panoply of Milton goes for nothing. But even if we leave out the grosser absurdities and keep to *Jonah*, the insensitiveness is crass— *Jonah*, a tale with as few even pretended historical attachments as *Job*, grotesque in incident and surely not without a distinct, though of course edifying, vein of typically Jewish humour. Then turn to John. Read the dialogues: that with the Samaritan woman at the well, or that which follows the healing of the man born blind. Look at its pictures: Jesus (if I may use the word) doodling with his finger in the dust; the unforgettable ην δε νυξ (8:30). I have been reading poems, romances, vision-literature, legends, myths all my life. I know what they are like. I know that not one of them is like this. Of this text there are only two possible views. Either this is reportage—though it may no doubt contain errors—pretty close up to the facts; nearly as close as Boswell. Or else, some unknown writer in the second century, without known predecessors or successors, suddenly anticipated the whole technique of modern, novelistic, realistic narrative. If it is untrue, it must be narrative of that kind. The reader who doesn't see this has simply not learned to read. I would recommend him to read Auerbach.'

C.S. Lewis on Biblical Criticism – Part 4

C.S. Lewis, "Modern Theology and Biblical Criticism" (an essay Lewis read at Westcott House, Cambridge, on May 11, 1959).

2

For some people the healing and telepathic powers, as well as the post-crucifixion appearances, attributed to

Jesus seem supernatural, miraculous. However, if one questions others widely enough, one is likely to come across accounts of seemingly improbable events. I have heard of the ghost of a very young boy appear on the other side of a house's interior wall, which he did not normally 'cross', and sit in a chair there, announcing to an au pair, "I am James". The young lady did not know that the boy was a ghost, so, having descended the stairs, she asked her 'hostess' who he was. On an occasion when I was suffering considerably from back-pain in southern France, a local lady (Madame Poudou, in Lagrasse) offered to help. She held her hands for two or three seconds, without actually touching me, so that one was in front at the right level and the other behind my back, also at the right level; I was cured. The cure lasted for the rest of the visit. On other occasions, so-called fortune tellers have displayed amazingly detailed knowledge of their clients, which could not have been discovered beforehand. Their forecasts bore good correlation with what actually happened too. The only feasible explanation is telepathy. Just as curious is the account of Alec Guinness meeting James Dean by chance in a New York restaurant at the end of September 1955 and his saying to James, when he showed Alec his new Porsche, something like, "Don't get in that car tomorrow! You will be killed if you do." He drove in that car the next day and was killed. Not long after Jesus's ministry a certain Hanina ben Dosa was celebrated as a healer. This man claimed that he could tell from the fluency in his prayer if the patient would recover or not: telepathy (see note 7).

3

We learn in Ashton, 'Understanding the Fourth Gospel' (OUP, 2007) p. 214, not only this (m. San. 11: 5): 'The false prophet is he that prophesies what he has not heard and what has not been told him, his death is at the hands of men; the death penalty is prescribed for any prophet or dreamer who utters falsehood about Yahweh your God', but also this (b. Sanh. 43a): 'Yeshu [Jesus] was hung [crucified] on the eve of the Passover, at the end of a period of 40 days [significant number] during which a herald went forth and cried, "He is going forth to be stoned because he has practised sorcery and led Israel astray."' This has been dated to an individual who was dealt with during the Hasmonean period a hundred years earlier but it fits Jesus so well that one feels there has to be, somehow, a connection; John Ashton clearly felt there was one. The accusation of sorcery is effectively referred to by John in 10:41-2, ' "John [the Baptist] gave us no *miraculous* sign," they said, "but all he told us about the man is true." And many came to believe in him there.' The implication here is that the difference between the two was that what Jesus performed were miracles, whereas there were no such miracles on the part of John; sorcery, in other words, was the distnguishing factor. Leading Israel astray was, in fact, appearing to reduce the authority of the priestly authorities by attracting that authority to himself. This was encapsulated in the interchange in the Sanhedrin after the raising of Lazarus when Caiaphas said that all they had to do to solve the problem was eliminate just Jesus and everything else would be put right. Of course, he was correct to say all would be well because the teaching of Jesus took off and was spread very far and fast, although we are still waiting – and hoping, if not with bated breath – for the teaching to reach into every single corner of the world.

4

A very useful account of Caesar's commentaries and their background is provided by Professor F.E. Adcock in 'Caesar as Man of Letters' (C.U.P., 1956).

5

For an explanation of how the position of fish may be seen from the shore of the Sea of Galilee when the fisherman in the boat cannot see where the fish are, see Professor William Barclay's commentary (Edinburgh, 1975) on John, vol. 2, p. 281, where he uses information from the travel writer, H.V. Morton: "The catch here is not described as a miracle, and it is not meant to be taken as one. The description is of something which still frequently happens on the lake. Remember that the boat was only about a hundred yards from land. H.V. Morton describes how he saw two men fishing on the shores of the lake. One had waded out from the shore and was casting a net into the water. 'But time after time the net came up empty. It was a beautiful sight to see him casting. Each time the neatly folded net belled out in the air and fell so precisely on the water that the small lead weights hit the lake at the same moment, making a thin circular splash. While he was waiting for another cast, Abdul shouted to him to fling to the left, which he instantly did. This time he was successful. ... Then he drew up the net and we could see the fish struggling in it. ... It happens very often that the man with the hand-net must rely on the advice of someone on shore, who tells him to cast either to the left or the right, because in the clear water he can see a shoal of fish invisible to the man in the water.' Jesus was acting as guide to his fishermen friends, just as people still do today."

6

A strong challenge to claims that every word in the Bible is relevant today is presented by the Book of Leviticus, where the detail of what one should sacrifice in atonement for sins is so labyrinthine that one suspects pedantic scribes were at work very early on in the development of Judaism. If Jesus came to free the Jews from slavery to such law, it is abundantly clear that some of what the Bible says is what God, according to Jesus, had decided we should bypass.

Even stronger are verses 3-15 of chapter 11 in Paul's first letter to the Corinthians: 'But I wish you to understand that, while every man has Christ for his head, a woman's head is man [what poppycock in today's world!] as Christ's head is God [no Trinity here]. [4] A man who keeps his head covered when he prays [one may pray anywhere and at anytime, whether the head is covered or not] or prophesies brings shame on his head; [5] but a woman brings shame on her head if she prays or prophesies bareheaded; it is as bad as if her head were shaved. [If a person is shamed for some good reason, that makes sense, but for a part of the body, and not the whole person, to be shamed, is plain nonsense.] [6] If a woman does not cover her head she might as well have her hair cut off [a lamentable lack of logic]; but if it is a disgrace for her to be cropped and shaved, then she should cover her head. [7] A man must not cover cover his head, because man is made in the image of God [why not woman as well: is she inferior in some way? How should anyone imagine this anthropomorphic fancy true?] and the mirror of his glory, whereas a woman reflects the glory of man [what happens when a man is as ingloriously misled by ingrained habits of thinking as Paul is here? Does she reflect dark unreason?] [8] For man did not originally spring from woman [an extraordinary notion now, although not then]; [9] and man was not created for woman's sake, but woman for the sake of man [what about continuation of the species? Once again Paul fails to understand the logic of the situation]; [10] and therefore a woman must have the sign of her authority on her head, out of regard for the angels. [gobbledegook!]. [11] Yet in the Lord's fellowship woman is as essential to man as man to woman [right for a change!]. [12] If woman was made out of man, it is through woman that man now comes to be; and God is the source of all. [This last statement might require some qualification: God is the source of all that is good in human conduct and man the source of all that is wrong].'

[13] 'Judge for yourselves: is it fitting for a woman to pray to God bareheaded? [what happens if she is praying on her own, as Jesus seems often to have done?] [14] Does not nature herself teach you that while long hair disgraces a man [does it disgrace a Sikh for whom short hair is a disgrace?], [15] it is a woman's glory? For her hair was given as a covering [what is man's hair for?].'

It is true that this passage may have been a later addition from another hand but that hand is directed by a mind steeped in the scribal way of thinking that Jesus had come to end. What it states about propriety as to dress may have applied when the letter was written, but what it states about the superiority of the place of man before God, as compared with woman, is the opposite of what Jesus demonstrated in his treatment of everyone; the anthropomorphic mind of the writer demonstrates human fallibility with blinding clarity. The writer is often utterly wrong in this section, as also are those who considered the arguments here worth preserving, unless it was to show us all how wrong even the most respected human mind may be and how we should all think carefully before we decide to believe anything, which must, in turn, require us to examine carefully what we read in the Bible before we accept it as reliable.

7

A very interesting example of telepathic power in the area, a little while after Jesus, was exhibited by Hanina ben Dosa, as described in Wikipedia: 'Another tale states that, at the solicitation of Gamaliel II, Hanina entreated mercy for that patriarch's son, and at the conclusion of his prayers assured Gamaliel's messengers that the patient's fever had left him. This assurance created doubt in the minds of the messengers, who promptly asked, "Art thou a prophet?" To this he replied, "I am neither a prophet nor the son of a prophet; *but experience has taught me that whenever my prayer flows freely it is granted; otherwise, it is rejected.*"' This account makes it clear that an important part of Hanina's endowments was telepathic understanding of the condition of the patients for whom he was praying.

8

Kenny writes on p.6 about Heraclitus's "...three-book treatise on philosophy and politics, now lost, of notorious difficulty, so puzzling that some thought it a work of physics, others a political tract. 'What I understand of it is excellent,' Socrates said later, 'what I don't understand may be excellent also, but only a deep-sea diver could get to the bottom of it.'" The writer of the Gospel of John may well have found the challenge of understanding Heraclitus's works exhilarating – he will have known of the comments made by Socrates; he was the 'deep-sea diver' of Ephesus.

9

Vv. 3-8 are the ones favoured by Jehovah's Witnesses, in which those to receive the seal of God upon their foreheads are twelve thousand from each of the twelve tribes of Israel only, but v. 9 has, 'After that I looked and saw a vast throng, which no one could count, from all races and tribes, nations and languages, standing before the throne and the Lamb.' The Jehovah's Witnesses seem to lay less stress on this. However, precise numbers do not so obviously accord with what one would expect from an all-loving God, so the second part sounds more reasonable than the part stressed by Jehovah's Witnesses.

10

Motyer translates, p. 435, 'One assigned his grave/ his grave was assigned with wicked ones and with a rich one in his deaths.' He gives a very useful and full commentary on the verse which is continued on p. 436. It is quite clear that the criminals and the rich one are two different concepts: neither should be confused with the other. As it stands, the statement is a contradictory discord which only the crucifixion of Jesus resolves. Any argument that tries to explain otherwise would seem to be that of the wilfully blind. This verse has to be about Jesus, and no one else, yet it was written five or six centuries before the event which it foretells. God 'spoke' then, so we should believe that God 'speaks' now.

11

The Synoptics seem to have concentrated on Galilee; the source for Mark may have spent little time in the Jerusalem area – he might have been earning his living in the early days – whereas the source for John seems to have spent a considerable amount of time even in the High Priest's domain, which accounts for his version of the ministry lasting long enough to include three Passovers and not just the one at the time of the crucifixion which is featured in the Synoptics. As a result Mark's source may well not have known anything about the raising of Lazarus, which the Synoptic writers would almost certainly have included in their accounts if they had learned anything about it. Peter might have learned about it from John, the son of Zebedee, but seems not to have used it during his teaching or, if he did use it, it was not recorded on any piece off papyrus that came into the hands of the writer of Mark.

12

William Barclay, in his commentary (Edinburgh 1956, p. 39), describes the usual house in the area at that time as having a flat roof, reached by an external stairway, of turf, often luxuriantly grassed, laid on clay-thickened brushwood, supported by beams, set, perhaps, three feet apart. Digging a hole in such a roof would have been easy and the repair easily effected. One might note that Luke, who has the same story, writes of the roof having clay tiles. Luke shows that he is not only using Mark, but that he does not know, *and has not thought*, about the construction of Palestinian houses. Indeed, it is clear that Luke has not researched the evidence as well as he seems to think he has done at the start of his Gospel (1:3). Incidentally, if Luke had obtained much of his information from Mary, the mother of Jesus, as some people seem to think, he would surely have said so at this point, the very start of his Gospel.

13

The implied criticism in the question about fasting – a public display of adherence to rules – sounds likely, while the metaphor of not fasting when the bridegroom is still with them is echoed in John as well as elsewhere in the other Gospels. This fairly frequent criticism of

Jesus's failure to adhere to required religious practice is a useful guide to what Jesus must often have taught: 'The current interpretation of the law is totally unreasonable: the law was made for us, not we for the law.'

14

With regard to work it is worth remembering that Paul said earning one's living and not living solely off the generosity of others was an important contribution to the missionary effort. He is likely to have been copying Peter in this, while Peter seems to have had a family to support. Peter may well have missed much of Jesus's activity in the Jerusalem area because he probably needed to earn a living for a family as well as for himself. Thus, ties with fishing are likely to have been still operational, even if his brother Andrew were to become more and more responsible for keeping the business going.

We may take particular note of 1 Corinthians 9:5, as has been pointed out (p. 66 above): 'Have we not the right to take a Christian wife about with me, like the rest of the Apostles and the Lord's brothers and Cephas?'; although earlier, in 7:8, he says that it is well that he remains single and in v. 38 suggests that those who remain single do better. Paul would need to continue working to support his wife, if he had one. This continues with, 'Are only Barnabas and I bound to work for our living?' In 2 Thessalonians 3:8 we have: 'We did *not* accept anyone's food without paying; on the contrary, we laboured and toiled, day and night, *working* so as *not to be a burden* to any of you.' One wonders how many Popes have read this little piece about the Apostles having wives…? Of course, the Roman Catholic hierarchy, which expects congregations to support their priests so that they do not have to do paid work to 'earn a living', as did Paul, decided that to expect congregations to support wives and families, as well as the priests, might be too heavy a burden to impose on them. Hence was developed the rule of celibacy, which is inadequately explained by the curious notion that every priest is married to the Church already and so should not have another wife in need of attention, thus reducing the priest's time to attend to his flock.

15

The writer of John almost certainly knew Mark's Gospel and so will have known of this list, which he does not echo anywhere in his Gospel. He must have thought there was insufficient evidence to provide a definitive list. Twelve is too convenient a fit with the twelve tribes of Israel to tie the number of chief missionary disciples to such a traditional number both convincingly and precisely; it might have been a name for a group that did not, in reality, match that particular number, rather like the actual number of legionaries in a Roman legion never being the stipulated figure – more often, say, about

3,500, rather than the 'official' 6,000. A more reliable way of deciding who the special followers of Jesus were is, almost indisputably, finding out who is named in any stories. Mark names only Simon Peter, his brother Andrew, Judas Iscariot, and the sons of Zebedee, James and John, with any regularity. Levi, son of Alphaeus, a tax-collector, in whose house Jesus dined, is mentioned just once, in connection with the account of authorities complaining that Jesus defiled himself by eating with tax-collectors and sinners.

More curious are Paul's statements in I Corinthians 15:5-7: "...and that he appeared to Cephas, then to the twelve; afterwards he appeared to over five hundred brothers [no sisters!], all at the same time [the Ascension?] most of whom are still alive, though some have been laid to rest; after that he appeared to James [Jesus's brother], then to all the apostles; last of all, even to me, untimely born [he wished he had been one of the first disciples], he was also revealed." There seems to be a distinction between a traditional twelve and the apostles. There is no list in John, and one would have expected the witness to remember them all. He did not remember the parables, so perhaps he had no memory for those who were not otherwise sufficiently memorable; or, just as possible, the idea of a specially selected twelve, to be called apostles (missionaries, commissioned with special powers), was adopted later and then developed further after that.

16

Barclay, p 90, provides an alternative translation from the Septuagint that fits the explanation given here – the minds were dull already, not to be dulled at the command of God – while his analysis of background, on pp. 91-94, is keenly recommended. This alternative translation, however, does not accord with that given by Childs (p. 50). The apparent mistake in the original may be designed to alert the minds of hearers and readers to the divine origin of the message: the human error shows that there is a divine source that has been misinterpreted here.

17

Barclay, pp.174-8, provides a detailed exposition of this which is well worth attention.

18

The name Maccabeus, originally given only to Judas, the son of the Hasmonean Mattathias, who killed an apostate Jew, may have meant 'hammer', as in 'Scottorum malleus' or 'Hammer of the Scots', the name given to Edward I of England when he punished Scottish attacks in Northern England.

19

Mark 11:22-3 describes faith, when it is sufficient, as being able to have a mountain, which represented a difficulty, hurled into the sea, while Matthew (17:20-

1) has the description of faith no larger than a grain of mustard seed being sufficient to move a mountain – again representing difficulties – from here to there. The description of the tiny mustard seed as being able to grow into a large plant which would provide great benefit to many occurs in Mark 4:31-2 and in Luke 13:18-20. Luke knows the original use of the idea of the mustard seed but a cursory memory of Matthew's linking of the mustard seed, faith and removing difficulties has become confused in his mind and he has incorrectly changed the wording of the metaphor.

20

Qur'an, 'House of Imran', 60, translated by Arthur J. Arberry, has: "No; Abraham in truth was not a Jew, neither a Christian; but he was a Muslim." The added comment that Abraham was not a Christian, so astoundingly unlikely an idea, makes the intent of these remarks about Abraham clear: to promote the standing of the message of the Prophet Muhammad by demoting, or even denigrating, religions regarded as competitors. As so often, like the claims in the Bible, the claims in the Qur'an need supporting evidence, if they are to be considered justifiable.

21

Qur'an (Arberry), 'Women' 155, has: "…and for their saying, 'We slew the Messiah, Jesus, son of Mary, the

Messenger of God'—yet they did not slay him, neither crucified him, only a likeness of that was shown to them."

22

An extravagant example of development is the derivation of the English words 'safe' and 'whole', which actually have the same meaning in that what is safe will remain whole in the future while what is whole is so because it has been safe in the past. The root was the Indo-European word 'SOLWOS', the initial 's' becoming an 'h' in Greek (originally holwos, the 'w' being a digamma, and then holos when the digamma was dropped) which might be thought of as 'Wholos' – whole – and the Latin word was 'SALVVS' from which the French developed their word 'sauf', which is related to the English word 'safe'.

23

There are references to Horeb as the mountain of God in Exodus 3:1, where Moses sees the burning bush, and in Deuteronomy 33:19, where 'They will summon peoples to their mountain.' We have also Psalm 48:1, where God's holy mountain is described as fair and lofty, and again, in Isaiah 25:6, we have a repeat of the wonderful picture in which the predicted heaven is a banquet on the mountain for all the peoples. There follow the even more splendid verses 7-9, which are worth reading. We have also Ezekiel 17:22-4, where God is written of as going to plant a slip, a tender shoot, from the lofty crown of the cedar on the highest mountain in Israel, where it will grow and become a haven for birds of every kind – all the peoples of the world, in other words.

24

John's version (2:19) of what Jesus perhaps laughingly said runs: 'You go ahead now and destroy this temple and I shall raise it up in three days.' The writer goes on to explain that Jesus was referring to his own body and not the building. His further suggestion that the disciples remembered this when Jesus reappeared after the crucifixion is an unwarranted deduction on his part, as there is no known evidence for this being the case.

25

There may be, sadly, no mention of an Alexander anywhere else in the New Testament, but reference to a Rufus is made by Paul in his letter to the Romans 16:13, where he is singled out for special recommendation. This Rufus must have been based in Rome, so the readers are likely to be in Rome: the writing of the Gospel may well have taken place in Rome too. There is another reference of interest in Acts 13:1, which mentions a 'Simeon' (=Simon) who is described as 'niger', i.e. as of swarthy appearance, and so probably from Africa. This may be the same man. This occasion may have been like those times in the army when the sergeant, or even corporal, would announce: 'I need three volunteers: you, you, and you!', as he pointed his commanding finger.

26

At St Giles Fair in Oxford on a Tuesday in September 1946, it took me, a slim eleven year old, 45 minutes to travel – along the middle – from the northern end of St Giles to the southern end, a distance of not much more than a quarter of a mile.

27

This may be based to an important extent on the remark made about Jesus when he was reported as having said (John, 8:56): 'Your father Abraham was overjoyed to see my day; he saw it and was glad.' The Jews protested (v. 57), 'You are not yet fifty years old. How can you have seen Abraham?' The misallocation of who saw whom suggests that this interchange is probably based on fact. However, it is very possible that Jesus looked older than he actually was, particularly if he was deformed. One might note, in passing, two points. When Jesus was engaged in discussion with those who were irremediably against his teaching he deployed ideas and arguments that muddied the waters rather than cleared them, while he, in this interchange, also makes it clear that time is of this world but has no effect in God's domain where past, present and future seem to be all one.

BACKGROUND CONSIDERATIONS

—

When researching for historical facts one needs always to be aware that the facts may not be exactly as they have been portrayed. For instance, how accurate is the picture presented in the Domesday Book of 1086 based on a survey dated to 1085? According to the entry for Oxford there were, out of a total of 946 houses, 478 so waste and destroyed that they could not pay geld. (Ruth Fasnacht, 'A History of the City of Oxford', Basil Blackwell, 1954, pp. 17-18). We are informed that the castle was built in 1071 – seven years before the White Tower in London, p. 20 – with its tower of the church, St. George-in-the-Castle, dated to 1074 (p. 22). Robert D'Oili (p. 23), also built the Grandpont Causeway of twenty-three bridges from the south, Pettypont, now Magdalen Bridge, in the east and Hythe Bridge (central west). Oxford had become unimportant and relatively uninhabited with the unification of England under Cnut in 1016, with access hampered by water, water everywhere. As a result, after the Norman conquest, Robert D'Oili was handed an economically useless area for him to administer. He must have been very enterprising; he seems to have been the first property whizz-kid. So successful was he that from being a dead-end backwater Oxford became so significant that two religious houses were established early in the twelfth century: St Frideswide's Priory and Osney Priory, later to be an abbey (1154), founded respectively in 1122 and 1129. It was increasing litigation between these two houses in the second half of the twelfth century, mostly about entitlement to tithes, one assumes, that attracted law students to Oxford. Even earlier, a schoolmaster, Theobald d'Etampes, began offering his teaching services in Oxford in 1095 (History of the University of Oxford, Clarendon Press, vol.1, p. 1). A prominent exponent of self-promotion, such as he, would not have come to a place which lacked widely known importance. Oxford was almost certainly in far better shape than the picture presented in Domesday suggests. The compilers of that survey will have had an easy and probably profitable relationship with Robert D'Oili. The Domesday picture of Oxford may have been true in 1066 but was almost certainly not true at the time when the record was made.

Much more recently we have been reminded often of how close the world was to nuclear war when, in October 1962, the Cuban missile crisis was at its height. During that, the sides involved were fully aware of what was going on. However, far less well-known, in the middle of November 1960, one dark evening, the nuclear-bomb-loaded B52 American planes were circling Brize Norton runways, ready for 'instant' take-off: according to an insignificant entry in a May 1961 issue of the *Daily Mail*, the computers had gone wrong. Luckily, the fault was discovered before catastrophe occurred. It is when people do not know what is going on that the dangers may be worse.

'Facts' are not as reliably true as they are so regularly believed to be. Not for nothing did the Jews require two witnesses for something to be accepted as 'fact'. What we read in the Gospels should, it is very clear, be assessed with considerable care.

APPENDIX ONE

—

An example of traditional commentary on the Gospel of Mark, 7:18, where Jesus asked them, "Are you as dull as the rest?" is appended here (commentary in italics):

'The unbelief of the disciples grieves Jesus'. This is possible. *'Their spiritual dullness amazes him even more* (noted in Mark 16:14)'. This must be nonsense, for Jesus was a communicator among the very best ever, while his understanding of mental processes going on in people when he was with them was just about unequalled. The commentator is, therefore, implying Jesus is incompetent. *'For this is the quality that also distresses him in the Pharisees (3:5)'* – actually one should take vv. 1-6 here, not just v. 5. *'The chief thing obvious to a modern reader is the utter failure of the disciples*

to understand even His simplest utterances.' It is quite ridiculous to claim that Jesus had failed as lamentably as this in teaching disciples he had specially chosen; he was one of the most remarkable teachers ever to exist. *'They consistently and crassly misinterpreted Him, taking his words in the most crudely literal sense (cf 8:16)'* [where Jesus was talking, in effect, about the teaching of the Pharisees as if this 'yeast' were concrete bread when the concern of the disciples was that they had nothing (no bread) to eat at that moment]. Cross misinterpretation by his pupils cannot be anything but an impossibly stupid libel on Jesus's ability to teach. *'Admittedly this was before the coming of the Spirit, the great interpreter (Jn. 14:26): and the same blindness is, according to Paul, still seen in 'natural' unconverted people (2 Cor. 3:14).'* Jesus's disciples had been 'converted', so these remarks are totally out of place.

The tendency to accept as right the traditions observed by previous commentators is exposed as fundamentally disastrous here. This commentator referred to the Gospel of John. If he had taken into account what one learns there, he would have understood that the relationship of Jesus with his disciples was rather different from the picture presented by Mark. It is also clear that Jesus's sense of humour, which must have been almost irrepressible, has been missed by too many commentators. A great teacher is a showman, an actor, sometimes a comedian, as well as possessing that sort of humour and engaging understanding of an audience that disarms criticism and dissipates any animosity. Jesus was a teacher sans pareil, while his sense of humour was so omnipresent that an enormous amount of what might seem to be severe criticism is almost certainly gently smiling correction, not harsh reprimand.

APPENDIX TWO

—

Perhaps one should start with the meaning of the term 'Economics'. The 'nom' element is the same as that in the fifth book in the Bible called 'Deutero**nom**y', Second Laws. The Greek word 'nomos' included among its meanings the idea of good regulation, as associated with the almost fabled Greek statesman, Solon. The defined and rigid regulations attributed to Draco, entailing harsh punishments, were termed 'thesmoi'. The other Greek word is 'oikos', meaning 'house'. Economics is concerned with good regulation in household management, following Xenophon, then management of a region, of a country, of a world, or, perhaps we should think, of everything. Where and when people work together to produce anything, goodwill is of great importance. For instance, an industrial strike, which effectively suspends regulation in a deliberate demonstration of ill-will, while curtailing or ending industrial operations, also reduces the size of the economic cake we all share by stopping the production of what people want. This so-called industrial action – it is very deliberate inaction, not action – arises from perceived injustice or ill-will in the work-place and generates ill-will elsewhere, as well as damaging the economy. Perhaps one might think of an industrial strike as a form of warfare; it is certainly the result of weak management, which has failed to understand the employees, as well as the real structure and operations of the enterprise which it is responsible for managing, and which has not managed to work out how to make itself understood by the members of the workforce; perhaps, if the people discharging managerial responsibilities had to forgo some of their remuneration when those they were responsible for were on strike, they might try a little harder to understand the situation and communicate better, by *listening* as well as trying to explain.

The misunderstandings are too often exacerbated by the dishonest use of tendentious language on one or more sides. Far too few people have been educated well enough to consider adequately and dispassionately all sides to an argument in a dispute; they have not learned why and how the facts they learn are labelled as such nor why, how, when and what facts should be used in an argument or an attempt to solve a problem.

A war, which is a failure in political management, on one or more sides, destroys and so, in effect, does a strike. The teaching of Jesus is about the benefits for all that derive from peace and goodwill and positive motivation. An earlier example was provided by the economic prosperity conferred by the Pax Romana. We should behave so that there is imaginative co-operation in all things!

The 'oikos' element, in the study of Economics, comes to comprehend the apparatus, the machinery, which produces goods and services, and helps in the transmission and exchange of those goods and services. If there are more goods and services of the best possible quality which people need or desire, so long as there is not an unwanted (hence wasteful) surplus and so long as the production systems are not socially or environmentally unfriendly nor wasteful in any way, that is thought to be better than there being fewer goods and services which are perceived as being needed or desired, particularly when the quality of those goods and services is inferior to what is hoped for. Obviously, the quantity and quality of the goods and services both matter, and in producing these goods and services goodwill is a very important factor.

If people are to produce goods and services that are as excellent and plentiful as needed and desired, those engaged in the production need to be equipped with the right skills and attitudes, and kept in good enough health to carry out the necessary work to the desired standard. This involves, firstly, the element of education, including the inculcation of the right attitudes and habits (social goodwill, as taught by Jesus, being part of this, as well as comprehensive understanding; rote learning of facts and formulae is not enough), which occurs in home, school, further education establishments, social environments and any ventures chosen by a 'subject' for further investigation or experience. Without the vital element of education being properly attended to, economic failure, at least in some degree, is to be expected. Secondly, if the ability of the appropriately skilled individuals is restricted by illness or other physical disability, the economy suffers, so the next vital element is provided by a health service. Once again, for proper functioning, goodwill is an essential part of the healing process. Thirdly, there is the very necessary element of 'law and order' which good-will ensures far more effectively than any other force, such as policemen or soldiers. Fourthly, there is another element, which is often in the form of 'money', which is a means of relating the value of one or more lots of goods and services to another or others, so that a sort of exchange may take place at different times yet to be determined. As an aside, one may note that it is desirable there is confidence that any money received will be safely kept in the right hands and at a later date be sufficient to obtain something roughly equivalent in value to that which was given earlier in exchange for that money. Money is a confidence 'trick': so long as it continues to con us, it functions fairly well … or should.

However, money may be likened to grease or oil in an economic engine: enough is needed in all the appropriate places, while too much anywhere might lead to clogging or a reduction in economic activity. Of course, as has been implied, too little money anywhere leads to that part of the economy ceasing to function adequately. In all this, motivation is very important, and, if there is perceived to be any element of unfairness, work suffers as a result of deterioration in the underlying motivation. A very important part of positive motivation is goodwill.

One might think of the sharing out of money in all this, as it is with money that we obtain our share of the economic cake. If any group of people manages to appropriate to itself more than what is perceived by others as a fair share of the economic cake, particularly if their machinations result in a reduction in the cake's size or quality, this is seen as unacceptable, and is, as a result, counter-productive. They might also think that the systems which allocate top-rewarded jobs seem too often to be manipulated by small groups of self-serving people for their own and their own groups' benefit.

Envy, any sense of injustice and jealousy, damages the spirit of co-operation which all best practice needs. Jesus teaches us to obliterate injustice with well-argued goodwill, and the observance of just principles, which automatically accompanies that, so that we all work better and far more productively together. When any person or group of people is perceived as appropriating to itself a greater share of the cake than is fair, ill-will is engendered and productive motivation reduced, as noted in the previous paragraph; one may be reminded of that occasion when, because a group of people operating in the Temple precincts were appropriating to themselves and their superiors quite inappropriate quantities of money, Jesus demonstrated his disgust at this selfish stupidity by overturning the tables at which they were indulging themselves in their extortionate practices. As another example, some people suspect that the self-reward systems that apportion so much money to some people at the top of a variety of enterprises, financial ones in particular, should be considered unacceptable and counter-productive. They might also think that the systems which allocate top-rewarded jobs seem too often to be manipulated by small groups of self-serving people for their own and their own groups' benefit. This manipulation is not perceived as such by those who practise it: we may be sure they believe their way of working is the best available.

To recapitulate, Jesus teaches us to obliterate injustice with well-argued goodwill, while observing what people in general feel are just, equitable principles. We should all then work better and far more productively together.

APPENDIX THREE

—

One may survey everything with a background principle that this world, in which we live and have our being, is the only one we can manage fully to understand. St Thomas Aquinas seemed to think in similar terms. About God we cannot, as far as we can tell, know anything directly in normal material terms. Even the existence of God, it would seem, we can only infer, not prove, from any evidential data, internal or external, which we may chance upon. However, this world is a world in which everything is relative to everything else: nothing is absolute.

Scientists try to find out how we can arrive at an understanding of how everything works and how everything came into existence. Science is made up of theories which are suggested by and worked out from analyses of evidential data. Science is always open to change; there may be analyses of new evidential data which lead to changes in current theories or suggest new theories; there may be new analyses of previously available evidential data which suggest changes should be made to current theories or which even suggest new theories.

Nothing is either stable or absolute. Not surprisingly, there are some people who want to find something which might seem to them to be both stable and absolute, hence one of the reasons for some people wanting to believe in a totally different world beyond this one, one which may be imagined to be both stable and absolute. Because our genes are, generally, programmed to make us struggle to stay alive, whatever the challenges, there is also a desire to live forever, which generates hopes that this different world may be an eternal one for us to continue living in when we die. That many of us have to act in different ways to 'earn' a place and to survive in this world, which is the one we know, has given rise to theories that most of us have to earn a place in the next world, which we do not know, by living in the right way in this world. Hence, there is enormous concern with forgiveness, in some religions, for misdeeds that might otherwise seem to disqualify people from being allowed a place in the next world.

In addition to these arguments, there is the apparent principle that everything that happens in this world is caused by, or has its source in, something else. Lucretius wondered what would happen if someone threw a spear at the edge of space, away from what was seen as the centre of space; he calculated that it would either be stopped by a barrier beyond which there would be, by implication, something else or it would travel further. Somewhat similarly, it is felt by some people that there has to be a cause for the existence of this world: a Big Bang is not enough, even if there is an eternal cycle of big bangs; something has to have caused this and this has to be, by implication, something absolute and not anthropomorphic or material in any way. The existence of an 'absolute' was envisaged by the Greek philosophers, Heraclitus and Xenophanes. If there was just the one big bang, what was going on before the big bang? How is there nothing one moment and then something the next? As Lucretius thought of it, if the world we are experiencing is not eternal, then it would already have ceased to exist.

It is clear that Science, however it may be regarded, is vitally important for our understanding of how we should care for this world, which theists believe God has entrusted to us to look after. There may be people who see Science as grim and destructive, but they are dangerously in error because it is the *people* who use or abuse Science who do good or ill; Science on its own does not do anything. Similarly, Religion should not be seen as a threat to scientific study or endeavour, although some of those who have certain religious beliefs, may try foolishly to disparage Science or even argue against what seems to have been incontrovertibly established by convincing and clearly logical analyses of evidential data. Religion does not do anything; it is individual people who actually do things. When the precise connections between creeds and what people do are confused, while addressing problems, it is unlikely that there will be any good sense in the conclusions reached.

An example of how error may arise is provided by the game of football. For some it is 'the beautiful game' while for others there is no beauty in it nor anything of interest. It is a game that has been attended by terrible disasters caused by unruly behaviour or inadequate safety measures, or marred by poor conduct on the part of some players, sometimes feigning injury to imply foul play or inducing a player of the opposite side into unintended foul play. Such acts are not beautiful and bring disgrace on both players and teams. These faults are not the fault of the game nor, usually, its rules, but of the players. An outsider might blame the game, just as some critics blame religion for misdeeds such as, in the distant past, the sale of indulgences or the Albigensian Crusade. It is people who are responsible for their actions, which may be the result of disgraceful misinterpretation of religious tenets; it is not a religion or its tenets that are primarily responsible.

Similarly, there may be false religions or false religious statements or writings. The fact that some statements or claims are wrong does not mean that all are wrong. A claim that one has debunked religion without explaining exactly what and how is wholly inadequate. If one has managed to debunk one particular religion, that does not mean one has debunked every other religion too. If one has debunked a tenet or two of a religion, that does not mean one has debunked the rest of that religion. Some claims seem to display arrogance and laziness.

Let the scientists continue their vital work and let the theists or deists survey everything that there is and try to arrive at an understanding of what there may be beyond or outside the material world which we think we know. We cannot, with our finite minds, *know* that there is *nothing* beyond or outside our experience of this world, but we may certainly look for evidence that there may be something else, spurred on by the knowledge that in Science there are instances when the existence of something unobserved and possibly unobservable, can be inferred from evidential data. We may find we are able to infer the existence of God from our analyses of the available data.

Agnosticism would seem to be much more defensible than atheism but, even so, there are pieces of evidential data which may plausibly be construed as supporting the idea of the existence of a God who loves us all, regardless of how well or badly we manage our lives while we are here.

Some people will know that a writer, Ved Mehta, as an undergraduate at Balliol in 1956-9, who had been blind since he was four years old, could sense where things were as he meticulously 'measured' his way round the College and other places. He found waste-paper baskets more challenging than many other things. We might, in a metaphorically comparable way, be able to sense, somehow, that God is there with us. But even the existence of God we can only infer, not prove, from the evidential data available to most of us. Ved could not see the things of which he sensed the existence, but he could pick his way successfully through and past the challenges with this sense of the existence of things which he could not actually see. Perhaps we can, in comparable fashion, sense that God, whom we cannot see, is there, and then pick our way through life's challenges with help from that sense.

APPENDIX FOUR

—

Until now, it would seem, theological scholars have not arrived at a confident consensus about what Jesus was really like, nor precisely how, nor exactly what, he taught. As an instance of this one might consider the Kingdom about which Jesus is said to have spoken so much; this particular problem is more easily addressed by looking in Isaiah (2:2-5 & 11:1-9) and finding the very simple description of this *universal* kingdom, which springs from Judaism (via Jesus) and in which goodwill conquers every tendency to quarrelling and war in every nation upon earth: this Kingdom is *heaven* on *earth*.

It might appear that the dread hand of centuries of traditional scholarship has subconsciously inhibited fruitful exploration. Psychological motives, for instance, whether centred in people or culture, have not always been taken into account sufficiently: when Jesus called the almost uncontrollably impulsive Simon 'Cephas' ('rock', implying immovable stability) he will have been jesting, at least to some extent, and not being *completely* serious. When he called James and John, the younger sons of Zebedee, 'Sons of Thunder', Jesus was almost certainly joking; they were very quiet, as a perusal of John's Gospel, which was dependent on the evidence of the younger of the two, and of Acts of the Apostles shows. History may be about people, deeds, geography, climate and the intervention of disease and other natural events, but it is also about the motives and cultural effects involved too.

An historian has to try to see matters in the way that the people at the time saw them, so as properly to understand, interpret and then work out what happened when filling in any gaps left by inadequate evidence. As an instance of this it could be noted that that perceptive scholar, Professor E.P. Sanders, in 'Jesus and Judaism' (SCM Press, 1985), in which the reasons for the execution of Jesus are examined, seems to have placed insufficient emphasis on the statement claimed to have been made by Caiaphas in John 11:50, after the raising of Lazarus, that it would be beneficial if one man were to die to save everyone else: the effects of the raising of Lazarus were perceived as dangerously promoting the power and influence of Jesus over that of the religious authorities. Here, clearly stated, is a reason for the religious authorities' desire to eliminate Jesus. The resulting crucifixion of Jesus fits a record in the Babylonian Talmud, which some date to the Hasmonean period. We may be sure that it was Jesus who was crucified and not someone else, as some have claimed; in this instance the authorities would not have crucified the wrong person by mistake as Jesus was clearly too well known.

This very minor lapse in the reasoning of Sanders is probably due to his according the different accounts in the New Testament more or less equal status as to validity. One may see that the accounts in Mark, followed for the most part by the two later Synoptics, lack chronological coherence and reliability, whereas the accounts in John's Gospel have very strong eyewitness support for accuracy, and should, therefore, be preferred when there is disagreement. When this is done, we are in a much stronger position to reach that coveted consensus. We can do that by examining, in greater detail, the background of the writer of the Gospel, the character, actions and experiences of the eyewitness, and then establishing how the writer worked with the eyewitness to produce the Gospel.

The importance of determining who the writer and author of the Fourth Gospel is may be found in the works of two very different scholars: Geza Vermes notes on p. 18 of 'Jesus in the Jewish World' (SCM

Press, 2010), that the writer of John's Gospel presents Jesus as an other-worldly, super-terrestrial redeemer figure, missing the fact that the stories in the Gospel depict the exact opposite to that; Professor Bauckham says on p. 12 of 'The Testimony of the Beloved Disciple' (Baker Academic, 2007) that John's Gospel was written by a theologically creative and literarily skilled author who produced a distinctive version of the story of Jesus. The fact that this version is so distinctive makes it clear that one needs to establish why it should be so, and that Bauckham's conclusion that this Gospel was written by a Jerusalem disciple of Jesus may not fit the internal evidence in the Gospel quite as well as he believes.

John, the writer of the Gospel, could not only read but, presuming he did not use a scribe, which is a possibility, could also write. Writing then was a special skill; many people could not read but even fewer actually wrote. He shows he knew and must have enjoyed the almost insurmountable intellectual challenge of the philosophical works of Heraclitus, who had lived and died in Ephesus more than 500 years before Jesus was crucified. Nearly all of what Heraclitus wrote is now lost, but it is very likely that all was available for study then and there will have been other works *about* Heraclitus which are now lost. We can deduce this as we recognise the words of Heraclitus in the beginning of the Gospel. Delphic was an adjective that Heraclitus applied to himself, according to John Burnet in 'Greek

Philosophy: Thales to Plato' (Macmillan, 1914), and he was challenging the reader to discover the inherent though hidden meaning. Much of John's theology seems to be of the same ilk. Heraclitus had stated that there was a great Word which held forever and in accordance with which all things came about (see note 1). This matches very closely the declaration with which the Gospel begins. Another pointer might be the emphasis placed on the vital importance of love for one another towards the end of the Gospel, which could be seen as linking with Heraclitus's interest in harmonious balance being better hidden than openly displayed; harmony is of fundamental importance to Heraclitus.

In the Gospel the writer also displays very detailed knowledge of Hebrew Scripture. His use of the idea of Jesus being the light of the world, for instance, echoes the story of creation in Genesis, when God declares, "Let there be light...", and separates the light from the darkness. The Gospel writer alludes to this next when he declares that the darkness did not overcome the light. He had read widely, we may deduce, in Philosophy and, apparently, in Theology such as it was then. All this makes it quite clear that the writer could not be the John linked with Peter in Acts 4:13 where the two are described as uneducated common men; it would seem almost impossible that the writer of this Gospel could be viewed as at all uneducated, whatever the circumstances: the writer could not have been the son of the fisherman, Zebedee, the disciple who is linked so regularly with Peter; however, this son of Zebedee was almost certainly the witness. His brother, James, may have been executed by Herod Agrippa in 44 AD, but John is cited by Paul as a pillar of the Church in his letter to the Galatians 2:9 which, if this were written in 48 AD, would preclude John's having been executed at the same time as his brother; indeed, probably seeing the hostility building up, John may well have departed for Ephesus, when not with Peter elsewhere, even before 44 AD. He knew, at least intuitively, that his mission was to be a witness to the life of Jesus and he could not do that easily if he were in prison, and not at all if dead.

If the writer was acquainted with philosophical works and also had detailed knowledge of Hebrew Scripture, we may assume he was a man of leisure, a man of means. His apparent knowledge of Judaism and its Scriptures suggests that he was a member of a wealthy Jewish family. There may have been a good number of Jews in Ephesus then, although the evidence for this is sparse. The lack of evidence might be due to the strength of Greek philosophical thinking which will have lessened the appeal of a less obviously rational corpus of beliefs, thus discouraging any open display of adherence to them. Artemis, with her famous temple there, might have been something of a deterrent too. However, a reference to a synagogue in Ephesus is made in Acts, 18:19 where Paul argued with Jews, which is evidence that there were enough of them there to warrant an address by Paul. A further point that is very indicative of a scholarly mind, is the writer's interest in the use and implications of numbers. The work of a German scholar, M.J.J. Menken, was noted by Professor Richard Bauckham in the last chapter of 'The Testimony of the beloved Disciple'. The number of fish, 153, in the so-called 'miraculous' catch of fish in the last chapter of John, is a triangular number (base 17), while the number of syllables in the Gospel's prologue (1:1-18) is 496 (the 'IO' of John being taken as one syllable, as in the English 'yo') echoed by the 496 words, it is claimed, in the last chapter, vv. 1-23, which number is not only a triangular number (base 31) but also a perfect number in that it is the sum of all its factors, omitting 496 itself. The very extensive numerical gymnastics revealed by Menken and noted by Bauckham are remarkable and demonstrate that the writer moved in a totally different milieu from that of Jesus and his disciples.

As a student of Philosophy, and knowing well the Greek philosophers' disdain for the credibility of the traditional stories of Greek gods, as described in the works of Homer and Hesiod, the writer is likely to have been suspicious of supernatural or miraculous accounts in Jewish Scriptures and to have distrusted even more any claims about the supernatural or miraculous powers said to have been possessed by Jesus. He is almost certain to have heard of these before he was himself converted to believing in the divine origin of Jesus's teaching. This conversion may have happened when he had the life-changing experience of meeting the witness, the son of Zebedee, who had been such a devoted follower of Jesus.

It appears that he wrote the Gospel late on in the life of the witness and, one may infer, as he describes himself as 'Presbyter' or 'Elder' in the letters attributed to him, relatively late on in his own life also, while he shows no personal knowledge of Jesus in his writings, whether in the Gospel or in the three letters; indeed, at the start of his first letter, he writes of the *message* he has *heard* from Jesus, which words do not imply personal presence at the delivery of that message. If the writer had known Jesus personally or been a believer in the teaching of Jesus at the time of Paul's long residence in Ephesus (around 55 AD, possibly), he would, almost certainly, have known Paul and probably been known to Paul. There is no evidence of this in the writings of Paul nor in the writings attributed to John, as when Paul writes in his letter to the Galatians (2:9) of John being a pillar of the Church, he is referring to John the son of Zebedee, the witness, who was regularly paired with Peter, and not to John the Elder. The writer's conversion to 'Christianity' may have come about later. Even more telling is the absence of any reference to the parables, which Jesus almost certainly used; we find these in the other three Gospels, but no reference is made to them in the Gospel of John. If the writer had heard Jesus telling them or even heard of them directly from a witness, we may be sure he would have mentioned at least one, and very probably several more. The writer might say he is giving a sort of parable (παροιμία rather than παραβολή) at the start of chapter 10, but this parable is quite different from those we remember in the Synoptics. This word for parable is used again in 16:25 & 29. As he did not include any parables in his Gospel, we may safely deduce he had not been a disciple of Jesus and, indeed, may well not have believed in the divine origin of the message until he had met the witness, who, for his part, appears to have had no memory for parables.

First, as the stories bear the stamp of coming from detailed eyewitness memories, we need to establish who that eyewitness might be. Chapter 19:35 of the Gospel states, concerning the flow of blood and water from Jesus's side after it had been pierced by the soldier's lance, "And *the one* who *has* (the use of the perfect tense suggests the witness is present while this is being written) seen this has testified this, and his testimony is true and *that man* knows he is telling the truth so that you also may believe." The 'that man' makes it clear that the writer is not the witness but that someone else is this all-important witness, who is almost certainly present while the writer is actually writing; the 'that man knows', where the use of the present tense is another indication that the witness is actually there, increases the likelihood of this contention.

It is the obvious honesty of the witness's manner, when he told the writer about what he knew of Jesus, that will have convinced the writer that what he heard was indubitably true. If the initial cause of the writer's interest in the witness was the witness's bringing an apparently dead man back to life at public baths in Ephesus, this will have suggested to him that miracles were possible after all, in spite of what he had learned from the Greek philosophers. The identification of precisely who the witness is, although he is not actually named to save him from possible persecution, comes in the last chapter of the Gospel, which was added as the final seal of trustworthiness. Zebedee, the father of the very youthful John, was not mentioned earlier in the Gospel, possibly because his wealth may well have derived from business dealings with the High Priest's household, but identification of the witness, although not actually by name, is now needed. It is clear from the careful naming of the participants and the detail in the account, that this chapter has been added to strengthen claims to authenticity on the part of the Gospel. That it has been added by the same writer is convincingly indicated by the sophisticated use of numbers – 153 and 496 – and the clear eyewitness base of the account. The witness was the youngest son of Zebedee.

A further point is that John, the son of Zebedee, is mentioned by name in the other Gospels and in Acts of the Apostles, but not by his actual name in this Gospel. So prominent a figure will have been present at many of the events – probably very nearly all, in fact – but is not mentioned by name in this Gospel. The most likely deduction is that he is the anonymous disciple occasionally mentioned in the Gospel, sometimes as the 'Beloved Disciple' and sometimes as just 'a disciple' or 'another disciple'. His not being named is almost a guarantee, as he must have been there, that he was the witness for the writer.

It may be noted that Peter Stanford, in 'Judas' (Hodder & Stoughton, 2015) on p. 34 says that "Most scholars now believe John's Gospel was written in the early years of the second century CE." This statement applies neither to John Robinson nor to Professor Richard Bauckham, while Professor C.H. Dodd believed that there are details in John's Gospel's account of the trial of Jesus that must have been based, in effect, on eyewitness testimony. Stanford also notes that the extent of the vilification of Judas in the Gospel, particularly when Judas is described as a thief, is probably unjustified: he has not allowed for the eyewitness, because of his extreme devotion to Jesus, being so imbued with implacable hatred for Judas that he saw the worst even when there was insufficient evidence for such beliefs. The simple-minded witness would not have been able to understand all the complications in the mind of Judas which had led to his mistaken betrayal. Stanford is, therefore, being unsound when he dismisses the accuracy and reliability of John's Gospel because of an almost certainly exaggerated picture of Judas. This account of Judas's thievish behaviour shows that the writer was not someone who had known Jesus and the other disciples: if he had, he would not have written this; he wrote it because he was so convinced by the manner and honest certainty of the witness's command of his memories that he felt every detail was truly remembered, even though he corrected the drift occasionally, as when he said Lazarus was dead, rather than asleep as the witness had reported.

The eyewitness was clearly different from the writer as to life-experience, character and mental abilities. He appears to have remembered little of Jesus's actual teaching, not even any of the parables, which will account for the High Priest and his entourage being so tolerant of the young disciple, as he was not, as far as they could tell, although they will have known of his associating with Jesus, being corrupted by that: he remembered nothing that mattered. They therefore saw no serious harm in such a young person associating with this otherwise unacceptable preacher, faith-healer and 'sorcerer'. On the other hand, the witness's memory of events, and even what people said during these, was amazingly detailed and apparently undistorted by either the passage of time or memory reformulation on his part.

We learn first about the witness when he is described as a disciple of John the Baptist and associating with Andrew, the brother of another fisherman, Simon, later to be called 'Peter'. These two had time to spend indulging in the latest trends: they were the younger members of relatively prosperous families, unencumbered with time-demanding work. It would seem that they were based in Jerusalem, very possibly in a house owned by the rich Zebedee. They are likely to have been responsible for the delivery of preserved fish from their family fishing businesses to wealthy people in Jerusalem. It would seem that the witness's being well known to the High Priest's household implies that it was that to which he was supplying the fish.

An important clue is provided in chapter 4, about the conversation with the woman of Samaria: the disciples had gone to buy food but the witness had not gone with them, so he did not count himself as one of them, for if he had he would have said that some of the *other* disciples had gone, so as to show that he thought of himself as a disciple too. He was evidently too young for that. We can tell that the witnessing disciple had spent an enormous amount of his time with Jesus, as, at the end of the last chapter, he says that if everything which Jesus had done were to be written down the whole world would probably not have room for all the books that would have to be written.

We now have useful information about the witness.

We may conclude that he was very young and had plenty of time on his hands, because he was the youngest and indulged son of a rich family, and, taking into account the amount of information he had, he was energetic, probably an habitual runner and driven by almost inexhaustible curiosity. So devoted to Jesus was he that the writer gave him, transferring the devotion actually felt by one to the other, the title 'Beloved Disciple'. The conclusion reached by some commentators, echoed in some references in the Synoptic Gospels, that Jesus called John and his brother James 'Boanerges' or 'Sons of thunder' because they were of fiery temperament, is almost certainly wrong: Jesus will have conferred this title in jest. We know that all relatively reliable accounts of John pictured him as quiet and reticent on public occasions.

The next problem is to determine how a probably very sceptical writer came to believe so overwhelmingly in the apparently supernatural powers of Jesus that he felt it imperative to write about them and the divine message of Jesus. This would seem to require not only complete confidence in the reliability and enormous importance of the memories of the witness, but also something extra to convert such a sceptical mind into believing that the apparently supernatural was genuinely possible after all. The resuscitation of someone who was, to all appearances, dead, as told in the Syriac history of John, would account for this. This is covered in 'Where is the Evidence', pp.16-17.

The advanced age of the witness, the advancing years of the writer coupled with the immediacy of the new information as well as the driving excitement that resulted, probably meant that, as some parts of the Gospel suggest, the writer wrote much, if not all, while he was questioning the witness. This would go some way towards explaining the quite impossible claim in the Syriac History that the Gospel was written in an hour. It is not just the 'corrections' noted in this book that support the thesis of the question-then-write-the-answer procedure, but also those occasions when the writer implies the presence of the witness while he is actually writing, such as when he uses 'we' (21:24) or in the words chosen in 19:35 ff.

There is an interesting slant on the writer's use of his knowledge: Psalm 22 starts with, "My, God, my God, why hast thou forsaken me?" which, although quoted as the words of Jesus on the cross by Mark 15:34, with v. 35 ('Hearing this, some of the bystanders said, "He is calling on Elijah."') adding authenticity, echoed in Matthew (27:46-47), are omitted in John's account of what took place, although John quotes the psalm when he refers to v.18 ('They share out my clothes among them and cast lots for my garments').

There is a useful outline of the thinking of Heraclitus on pp. 6-8 of Anthony Kenny's 'A Brief History of Western Philosophy' (Blackwell, 1998).

It should be noted that Ephesus is the traditional

place for the origin of the Gospel. The Syriac History of John places John, the presumed witness, in Ephesus, after his leaving Palestine. Eusebius records that there were two tombs there to two famous Johns. It is indeed probable that the Gospel originated in Ephesus.

APPENDIX FIVE

—

Personal confessions: as a child, who had begun
to develop disbelief in Santa Claus when he saw
'one' at an elementary school in Wellingborough
in December 1939 when he was just 5, I never wavered
in my belief in God. There was an earlier occasion when
our parents had decided on some outing on which I
wanted to go when the weather was too inclement to
allow this to happen. According to my mother, I prayed
that the weather would improve and that I said, when
it duly got better, "Good old God!" I never believed
that the sound of thunder was due to God moving his
furniture about – in the many resting places spoken of in
John 14:2? There was another occasion, a few years later,
after lights were out, when some treasured possession
fell from my dormitory bed, and my attempts to find

it were all in vain. I prayed to God that if I found it, I would always believe in him. I found it almost at once. On a similar occasion, but in broad daylight, when about ten years old, I discovered that the small thin black cartridge catch, belonging to the 9mm shotgun which I possessed, had fallen somewhere in a very extensive area of long grass. I did not pray consciously to God but my feelings were similar both before, when the object seemed irretrievably lost, and long after, when suddenly it was there clearly to be seen near the edge of that huge expanse of green.

Much later, in 1967, when studying Psychology as part of a course for the Academic Diploma at the Institute of Education, London, there appeared to be no room for freewill: everything was dependent on genetic inheritance and how that was programmed by and with life's experiences. There seemed to be almost no point in believing in God. It was becoming able to calculate or, perhaps, more accurately, believe, rather incoherently, how there might be, in spite of this extensive programming of genetic inheritance, freewill after all, that restored some sort of status quo ante, although freewill probably plays a much smaller part in our lives than many of us imagine. Repeated acquaintance with the 21st chapter of John, as well as with the rest of the stories, has buttressed that faith and still manages to keep it upright. But, like Ved Mehta in his care to avoid bumping into objects, I have, constantly, to keep my senses alert to the 'presence' of God to avoid bumping myself into disbelief.

A further consideration might be that there are occasions in the lives of people when something happens for which there seems to be no rational explanation. When such a thing happens it is not usually adjudged impossible or miraculous, but inexplicable. It would seem that, in a material world, every event which occurs in it should have a material explanation, even if we do not know at the time what that explanation might be. It might, therefore, be adjudged irrational to look for an immaterial explanation for something which is only inexplicable.

An exception to this rule may be occasioned by this possibility of freewill. Freewill appears not to be explicable in the terms of this material world; therefore, if it exists, it can be explained only by presuming the existence of something immaterial which 'operates' a material body. For example, an automobile, contrary to what its name seems to imply, does not move itself: it is operated by an entity which is completely different from itself. The explanation of freewill should be similar, it might appear.

The only apparent 'miracle', then, is the possibility of the existence of freewill. This implies that there is an immaterial power which could, or does indeed, induce change in material events, but that the process in any such change should be explicable in solely material terms.

The nearest to hell in my nightmares may have been that occasion, aged four or five, when any bodily movement plunged me into a starlit well and then jerked me back into my crouching position in the bed. Perhaps we have to live our earthly lives over and over again until we have lived one well enough. However, I *was*, eventually, granted dreamy respite from this 'yo-yo' existence before I actually awoke.

APPENDIX SIX

—

Detective work is needed when evidence is not clear enough. This book is an attempt to do some detection. We have an example of how this may be done using a work by Thomas Hardy. His poem, 'The Darkling Thrush', may be loved just because of the things which detective work may uncover. Indeed, what is revealed is probably already known intuitively by many. There is a preliminary draft of the poem, then the finished version which was published on 29th December 1900, the last year of that century.

We start with the preliminary version (see picture of manuscript). In this version one should note not just 'twig-lines', changed to 'bine stems' in the published version, but a number of words. 'Eye of day' echoes the idea of the eye being the light of the soul in the teaching of Jesus. We have 'crypt' for stowing buried bodies beneath a church, suggesting an inescapable end in a lifeless Hades. Most powerful of all we have the word 'morrowless': no future. The 'outburst' which follows is not just the sudden effect of this great sound, one might suggest, but the hope of bursting out from the constraints of what the sterile vision of the agnostic belief system seemed to offer. There are other interesting changes: 'paddock' has become 'coppice' and, even more telling, as already noted, 'twig lines' has become the far more effective 'bine stems'. The Gospel writers will have engaged in the same sort of developments; they wanted their message to be as memorable, as telling as possible.

This is the published version:

I leant upon a coppice gate
When Frost was spectre-grey,
And Winter's dregs made desolate
The weakening eye of day.
The tangled bine-stems scored the sky
Like strings of broken lyres,
And all mankind that haunted nigh
Had sought their household fires.

The land's sharp features seemed to be
The Century's corpse outleant,
His crypt the cloudy canopy,
The wind his death-lament.
The ancient pulse of germ and birth
Was shrunken hard and dry,
And every spirit upon earth
Seemed fervourless as I.

At once a voice arose among
The bleak twigs overhead
In a full-hearted evensong
Of joy illimited;
An aged thrush, frail, gaunt, and small,
In blast-beruffled plume,
Had chosen thus to fling his soul
Upon the growing gloom.

So little cause for carolings
Of such ecstatic sound
Was written on terrestrial things
Afar or nigh around,
That I could think there trembled through
His happy good-night air
Some blessed Hope, whereof he knew
And I was unaware.

We may note many things; however, we feel, first of
all, the bleak scene which confronts Thomas Hardy.
Apparent death is centre stage; paralysing cold pervades
the dying day in a dying century. But then, when we
read the last verse, we learn what matters. The poem
was written when Christmas carols, with their ecstatic
sounds, would have been ringing in the hearts and
minds of many people. Hardy demonstrates powerfully
in his novels that he was inescapably a realist and the
endings were often not the happy ones so many people
hope for. The carols of Christmas revel in a beautiful
world of escapism, seemingly alien to the real one he
knew so intimately. Our doubting Thomas, indeed,
in spite of having friends who had been ordained as
ministers in the Church and his attachment to church
life and ritual, seems to have been more or less agnostic,
as no one whom he knew had found the convincing
answers for which he was hoping. It is in this last verse
of the poem that the reader sees everything which

really matters: words such as 'carolings' ('carollings' in the draft), 'ecstatic sound', 'written on terrestrial things', 'blessed', 'Hope'; these words are the evidence. Hardy was enveloped by a feeling that the world, in which there was so much wrong, was without a God who cared, and without hope. He wanted to escape from the terrestrial world which he was surveying then and also the fantasy world of Christmas. He found a glimmering of light in the thrush's contribution to the dying light of day in that dying century; we know this indubitably because of two details: he wrote the word 'Hope' with a capital letter and then called this Hope 'blessed', which epithet is entirely theological in aura when set in this context. What does this prove? Hardy was yearning for a caring God in whom he could believe rather than the impersonal, immanent presence that might underly everything in the manner of the LOGOS of Heraclitus; he yearned for a world in which goodness and goodwill would prevail at the last. The way to God, proclaimed in Churches and propounded in theological books, appeared neither completely real nor sufficiently effective. He had not properly appreciated that God has given the responsibility of managing the world to us. He wrote the poem almost as a plea that a credible way to a credible God should be found.

Theology, as demonstrated in hymns and carols, as well as in much of what is preached, puts some reasoning people off and so deters them from finding the truth.

What is truth? Jesus seems to tell us, even if he had no chance to tell Pilate, that the truth is that there is only one God who loves his creation. What does this truth entail? Jesus may be telling us we should try to love likewise, showing this in our care and devotion for God's creation, because we have been given the task of maintaining and improving it. How might we do this? Perhaps we should follow the teaching of Jesus, as outlined in the parables and what we learn of him as a person in the Gospel of John. The Kingdom of God, for which we pray in the Lord's Prayer, is one in which *goodwill*, without there being the slightest scintilla of arrogance to mar the interpretation, *guides every action*, with every single mind open to instructions from God via the Breath of God, the Holy Spirit. The kingdom of God is within us, we have been told; we need to make it grow so well that there is no room for anything else. We bring this about with prayer and the actions that precede and follow that prayer.

REFERENCES

—

Adcock, F.E. (1956) *Caesar as Man of Letters*. Cambridge: Cambridge University Press.

Arberry, A.J. (1955) *The Koran Interpreted*. London: Allen and Unwin.

Ashton, J. (2007) *Understanding the Fourth Gospel*. 2nd edn. Oxford & New York: Oxford University Press.

Banner, M.C. (2009) *Christian Ethics: a brief history*. Malden, Mass: Wiley-Blackwell.

Barclay, W. (1956) *The Gospel of Mark*. 2nd edn. Edinburgh: St Andrew's Press.

Barclay, W. (1975) *The Gospel of John*. Revised edn. Edinburgh: St Andrew's Press.

Barclay, W. (2001) *The Gospel of Matthew*. 3rd edn. Edinburgh: St Andrew's Press.

Barton, J. and Muddiman, J. [ed.] (2001) *The Oxford Bible Commentary*. New York: Oxford University Press.

Bauckham, R. (2007) *The Testimony of the Beloved Disciple: narrative, history and theology in the Gospel of John*. Grand Rapids, Mich: Baker Academic.

Burnet, J. (1955) *Greek Philosophy: Thales to Plato*. London: Macmillan.

Cary, J. (2019) *The Sacred Art of Joking*. La Vergne: SPCK.

Childs, B.S. (2001) *Isaiah*. Louisville, Ky: Westminster John Knox Press.

Cole, R.A. (1989) *The Gospel of Mark* (Tyndale New Testament Commentaries). London: IVP Books UK.

Coleridge, S.T. (1930) *The Rime of the Ancient Mariner*. Oxford: Oxford University Press.

Fasnacht, R. (1954) *A History of the City of Oxford*. Oxford: Blackwell.

Freedman, D.N. [ed.] (2000) *Eerdmans Dictionary of the Bible*. Cambridge: W.B. Eerdmans.

Kenny, A.J.P. (1998) *A Brief History of Western Philosophy*. Oxford: Blackwell.

Marsh, J. (1991) *The Gospel of John*. London: Penguin.

Motyer, J.A. (1993) *The Prophecy of Isaiah: an introduction and commentary*. Downers Grove, Illinois: IVP Academic.

Robinson, J.A.T. (1976) *Redating the New Testament*. London: SCM Press.

Sanders, E.P. (1985) *Jesus and Judaism*. London: SCM Press.

Sanders, E.P. (1993) *The Historical Figure of Jesus.* Harmondsworth, Middlesex: Allen Lane.

Stanford, P. (2015) *Judas: the troubling history of the renegade apostle.* London: Hodder and Stoughton.

Vermes, G. (2010) *Jesus in the Jewish World.* London: SCM Press.

Vermes, G. (2006) *The Nativity: history and legend.* London: Penguin.

Wilson, I. (1984) *Jesus: the evidence.* London: Weidenfeld and Nicolson.

Woolley, A. (2021) *A New Vision: a fresh beginning.* Kibworth Beauchamp: Matador.

Woolley, A. (2022) *Where is the Evidence: finding the truth in the gospel of John.* Kibworth Beauchamp: Matador.

Hanina ben Dosa (2023) *Wikipedia.* Wikimedia Foundation. Available at: https://en.wikipedia.org/wiki/Hanina_ben_Dosa.